THE CONSTRUCTION OF ENVIRONMENTAL NEWS

The Construction of Environmental News

A study of Scottish journalism

FIONA CAMPBELL

Routledge
Taylor & Francis Group

LONDON AND NEW YORK

First published 1999 by Ashgate Publishing

Reissued 2018 by Routledge
2 Park Square, Milton Park, Abingdon, Oxon, OX14 4RN
52 Vanderbilt Avenue, New York, NY 10017

Routledge is an imprint of the Taylor & Francis Group, an informa business

Publisher's Note
The publisher has gone to great lengths to ensure the quality of this reprint but points out that some imperfections in the original copies may be apparent.

Disclaimer
The publisher has made every effort to trace copyright holders and welcomes correspondence from those they have been unable to contact.

A Library of Congress record exists under LC control number: 98074204

ISBN 13: 978-1-138-34257-6 (hbk)
ISBN 13: 978-1-138-34258-3 (pbk)
ISBN 13: 978-0-429-43970-4 (ebk)

Contents

List of Figures

List of Tables

Acknowledgements

I should like to thank Dr. Stuart Hannabuss without whose assistance this research would not have taken place and for his generous offer to compile the index. I am also indebted to Mhairi Hardie for her patience in sorting through the work and Grant Davidson for his technical expertise.

Grateful thanks go to all the journalists, both from the print and the broadcast sectors, who took part in the research, for their invaluable assistance. Thanks also go to the media librarians and the environmental and scientific specialists whom I interviewed for the work.

Finally, my thanks go to my friends, family and colleagues for their support and care.

List of Abbreviations

Codes for Journalists

EC1(n)	Environment Correspondent 1 (Newspaper)
EC2(n)	Environment Correspondent 2 (Newspaper)
EC(b)	Environment Correspondent (Broadcast)
EC(s)	Environment Correspondent for Sunday Newspaper
ENJ	Evening Newspaper Journalist
JEd	Journal Editor
LNA1	Local News Agency Journalist 1
LNA2	Local News Agency Journalist 2
LNJ	Local Newspaper Journalist
LRJ	Local Radio Journalist
LTJ	Local Television Journalist
NNJ1	National Newspaper Journalist 1
NNJ2	National Newspaper Journalist 2
NRJ1	National Radio Journalist 1
NRJ2	National Radio Journalist 2

NTJ	National Television Journalist
1	National Political Journalist
2	National Television Journalist
3	National Bi-media Journalist

Codes for Scientists

A	Veterinary Scientist 1
B	Veterinary Scientist 2
C	Agricultural Scientist
D	Zoological Scientist

Introduction

This book is based on a study carried out between 1992-1996 for a Ph.D degree. Its main purpose is to describe and explain the news process i.e. the journalistic methods used to identify a newsworthy issue; gather the information and construct the story that we read.

The main aim of the work is to explore the construction of environmental news and the information flow that takes place from a state of technical complexity, through retrieval by journalists, to mediation and dissemination via newspapers and television and radio stations. The relationship between science specialist and journalist or what Friedman (1986) calls the "symbiosis" i.e. the co-existence of two extreme, different professions for the single common aim, is examined.

The main arguments of the work are as follows: Environmental information is pluralistic and complex and has information meanings inherent in it. These are changed when journalists and the audience or readership interpret it. Essentially, environmental news is a version of "interpreted" environmental information. It is interpreted by the people who use it e.g. librarians, journalists, editors etc. Theorists in the field (Bagdikian, 1984; Ericson, 1987, 1991) support the view that the new technology involved in the news making process causes the creation of new information meaning structures (see chapter 2), but this work suggests that as environmental knowledge is retrieved and interpreted by journalists and news practitioners, the meanings which can be taken from this information, change. Therefore, the information changes according to how it is interpreted.

In chapter 2, it is argued that the flow of knowledge is influenced and redirected by the news process. Primary i.e. unmediated knowledge is altered into a popularised, commercial form and it appears to have been simplified due to the interpretive, journalistic process. In a news report the information may still be complex but it has been shortened and reduced to a series of manageable concepts, thus implying that some of the intellectual content of the original idea has been lost or changed i.e. the knowledge has been popularised. The work takes account of the extent to which the news is structured by the placing of values and meanings on the information, for example, issues of bias or the construction of the news product and its implications for the social construction of reality.

The study included a tri-faceted model which explained how this unmediated knowledge is altered and apparently simplified for audience consumption. The preliminary and secondary stages describe the interaction of the news media with sources of information. This model was designed at a time when very few Scottish journalists had access to electronic information and, unlike today, internet technology was not available. The research, therefore, does not take account of the implications of this technology for the news process and, if this is of interest, I would refer readers to the work carried out by David Nicholas[1] at City University which looks at the influence of electronic sources of information on journalistic information gathering (Nicholas, 1997). Parts of the model have been referred to in this text but the tertiary stage which depicts the different journalistic rule categories does not appear in its original form. Modifications had to be made in keeping with the book formatting but the tertiary stage has been adapted without losing the original meanings.

Chapter 3 examines the unique relationship between the journalists and the subject specialists. Due to the complex nature of scientific information, journalists refer to scientists during the construction and production of environmental news. This section highlights the "expert" as a journalistic information source and this is described by the preliminary and secondary stages of the model.

Chapter 4 provides a general introduction to the rules which journalists use to construct and produce the news. The possible origins of these rules, such as training, on-site experience, editorial and organisational policy and journalistic roles are investigated.

In chapters 5-8 a critique is provided for each rule category. It is suggested that if the news process (depicted by the tertiary stage of the model) could be described as a chronological statement the rule categories would be ordered in this way: evaluative, operational, constructional/interpretive and the editorial rules would be applied throughout. The editorial rules i.e. the procedures which affect editorial decisions are discussed in chapter 5.

The evaluative rules which journalists apply to potentially newsworthy environmental issues are found in chapter 6. This chapter includes the results of an experiment that required the journalists to prioritise five environmental case scenarios (see appendix I) according to their newsworthiness and leads to the categorisation of news. Issues such as journalistic news sense, news values and contextualisation i.e. the application of a template from a previous story to a current scenario are discussed at length.

The operational rules are ones which journalists apply to gather information and research background for the story. The information seeking strategies and sources which journalists consult are examined in chapter 7.

Chapter 8 looks at the rules used to interpret the information and construct the news. The constructional rules are specifically concerned with the writing and editing of the news product and the interpretive rules are identified as those which code and simplify the environmental information for the intended audience. This chapter also examines the results of an experiment, designed to reveal the exact information journalists select and reject during the news process, in which journalists were instructed to write up case 1 (see cases in appendix I) as a news story.

The examination of the rule categories reaffirms how decision-based the news process actually is.

The book is not an audience study and has not set out to reach any conclusions about if and how the media affects viewers, listeners or readers as other researchers have done (Bell, 1991; Morley, 1986; Tulloch, 1992). Rather, it aims to consider the audience not as an explicit, multi-faceted entity but as a collective body or mass which is defined by the perceptions of the journalist.

The data collected during the study was qualitative - samples of journalists were interviewed using semi-structured and in-depth methods. For the purpose of this book, where quotes are used respondents have been kept anonymous and a code, which describes the category of journalist, has been assigned to each one e.g. LNJ - local newspaper journalist. A full list of these codes can be found on pages ix-xi.

The book is an examination of the Scottish media. Where I have written "North-East", please note that this refers to "North-East of Scotland" (e.g. the table on page 68).

For the purpose of setting the work in context an overview of the theories and current issues pertaining to the media has been provided. It is also important to examine the role the media has played within the environmental movement in disseminating environmental information to the wider social groups. In order to do this, a brief overview of the environmental movement has been included in chapter 1.

Note

1. Nicholas, D. (1997) Journalism and the Internet: a study of the impact of the Internet on the information seeking behaviour of journalists. The preliminary results of this study may be found at: http://www.soi.city.ac.uk/~pw/ji_results.html

A Note on Methodology

The main findings which emerged from the study were concerned with the different types of rules that journalists apply when reporting news. A methodology was required which went beyond the conventional semi-structured interviewing technique. A hybrid form of ethnomethodology drawing on existing methods: in-depth interviews and discourse analysis evolved where each journalist was presented with a set of five potential news stories. This was termed as tri-lateral interactive discourse (T.I.D.). No formal interviews took place, at this stage, but each respondent was asked to take the researcher through the steps involved in reporting each case as news. An additional sheet of information (validated by scientists and experts) was provided for each case and the researcher was able to gauge exactly what information was used when the journalists wrote up case 1 as an actual piece of news. The results of this construction exercise demonstrated practically what the journalists discussed during the tri-lateral interactive discourse.

The cases (see appendix I) covered a wide range of environmental topics. These topics included: use of chemical pesticides in agriculture (1); the effects of air pollution on respiratory diseases (2); the development of a funicular railway through the Cairngorms (3); overfishing in the North Sea (4) and oil pollution in an inland estuary (5).

In addition, the respondents were asked to prioritise all five news stories according to their organisational values - discussion about this exercise can be found in chapter 7.

The methodology for the work was extensive and it is not appropriate for inclusion in this book. For those who are interested in reading more about this study I would direct them to the actual thesis which is referenced at the conclusion of this work.

1 News and Information

If journalism is the first draft of history, then, we can appreciate that, as with history, selection and interpretation will take place and that we are dealing not with a world of unassailable facts but with provisional accounts. (Eldridge, 1993, p6)

Environmental issues as topics of media concern

The environment as an area of interest and study has been evident for centuries (McDowell, 1993; McCormick, 1992). However, it was Rachel Carson's work on chemical pesticides in the 1960s which was instrumental in heightening media coverage of environmental issues. In the 1980s, coverage of environmental issues such as global warming, the ozone layer, oil pollution and nuclear waste became prolific and if one reviews the issues which the media championed for recently, it is evident that journalists are selective in the areas of the environment that they publicise. Burgess (1990) noticed that, for example, the issues about landscape and nature have not been represented as much as other areas.

The politicisation of the environment and the "greening of the media" in the late nineteen eighties has begun to stimulate more interest within these social science disciplines but they still remain resolutely silent about landscape. (Burgess, 1990, p7)

There is a wealth of information about the growth of the modern environment (McDowell, 1993; McCormick, 1992; Young, 1990; Lowe and Goyder, 1983). Many believe that interest in the environment as a subject of study began not at a particular point in time or with an explicit beginning but gradually and as a result of "a series of distinctive attitudes and values" (McDowell, 1993). However, Lowe and Goyder (1983) make the point that,

1

Environmental groups...are only one indicator of the wider social movement. Other indicators include the degree of sympathy expressed by non-environmental organisations, the burgeoning of environmental literature and the coverage of the environment in the news media. (Lowe and Goyder, 1983, p9)

They indicate something of the role of the media in the development of the environmental movement, revealing how much environmental information has been generated as a result of this publicity.

The Nineteenth century saw the rise of the first environmental interest groups, for example RSPB and RSPCA and also one of the first media reports on an environmental issue. The Times appealed for the preservation of our "old native flora and fauna" (1912)... (Lowe and Goyder, 1983, p20).

The latest environmental age (1960-present)

Theorists in the field have classified this period under many different headings e.g. the new environmentalism; the environmental revolution; the post material age etc.

Environmentalism in the late 1960s and early 1970s was characterised by doom laden warnings of imminent ecological disaster and demands for urgent, often drastic measures to avert this fate. (McDowell,1993, p17)

It was this period which resulted in the production of a phenomenal amount of environmental literature - information which is pluralistic and which exists in a number of different disciplines.

Environmentalism in the 1960s became explicitly political on not merely a national level but an international one as well.

The transformed movement - New Environmentalism - was more dynamic, more broadbased, more responsive and won much wider public support. (McCormick, 1992, p47)

It was this politicisation, together with the increase in the production of environmental information, which helped to create a greater public awareness about environmental issues. The information to be produced from this age (1960s to present) was complex and technical and scientific experts emerged as a result of the newly created specialisms within the cross disciplinary fields.

Rachel Carson's book, "Silent Spring", published in 1962 was instrumental, it is said, in communicating to the general public and causing an environmental awareness about pesticides and chemical insecticides. Carson's publication may be seen, therefore, as one of the first modern attempts to educate the public. Furthermore, it indicates that the 1960s and 1970s were periods of reactive environmental politics in comparison with the passive generations which had gone before.

The beginning of the 1980s reflected a downward trend for the environmental movement, but the mid to late 1980s caused a change in the ways of thinking about the issues and witnessed a move "from the periphery of the political agenda to the centre" (Young, 1990, p138). McDowell supports this view as she talks about the movement over the last four or five years,

> ...after a feverish rush of environmental activity in the late 1980s, recent trends suggest a general downturn in the green movement. This is reflected in a decline of environmental issues in government agendas and a fall in the fortunes of green political parties. (McDowell, 1993, p20)

The 80s was one of excitement and heightened publicity where the environment was concerned and this may be attributed, largely, to the media. However, it would appear that issues are losing their appeal and in recent years environmental issues do not seem so prolific. This argument is reinforced by the reduction in the coverage of environmental concerns in the media. Populist environmental policies like recycling and the purchasing of products without CFCs, have been much more widely implemented in our daily lives and the media take a lot of the credit for educating the wider social community i.e. the audience or readership.

Scientific specialists or experts who emerged from these environmental disciplines have now become part of people's awareness about the environment. These specialists are important sources of primary information for the media, as reporters interpret and repackage this type of information for the readership or audience.

How the flow of environmental information from source to media and media to audience, is established, will be considered later on.

3

The media as information providers

...Many people with little formal training in science have a compelling interest in all kinds of science...when non-scientists are looking for scientific information they turn to the mass media. (Friedman, 1986, p218)

The amount of environmental information which has been produced for mass consumption has increased dramatically, in recent years. It is possible that one of the factors contributing to this, is the mass media. It is undeniable that from the mid-60s onwards, a period of "environmental crisis" (Young, 1990), and a greater awareness about the environment has emerged, encompassing industry and education. The media, including print and broadcast news; the documentary film, current affairs criticism etc. have been, for the greater part, responsible for this. The Scottish Office report, "Learning For Life: A National Strategy For Environmental Education in Scotland" (1993) indicates that the majority of people receive their environmental information from the media.

The report draws on findings from the survey of Public Attitudes to the Environment in Scotland stating that the main source of environmental information for people is television with the only other main contender being newspapers. It is suggested that in comparison to news items on the environment, television programmes devoted to issues were more specific and, therefore, preferable.

> Television has had a major role in making many of the population environmentally aware. It has also increased understanding, although one might sometimes wonder if people who have been inspired to explore the real world outside for themselves are disappointed by what they find. (The Scottish Office, 1993, p32)

The report also takes notice of the fact that there has been a marked increase in press and magazine coverage of the environment and that there is need for the training of journalists to include how to cover environmental issues. It makes a further point that although the media is a useful way of transmitting messages to a large audience, the media are governed by ratings figures which have economic implications. The report, then, puts forward a strong case for using the media not only as a social educator but as a valuable source of environmental information.

Lowe and Goyder (1983) suggested that the media access sought by environmental groups leant towards the national "quality" newspapers

4

rather than television because of the specific audience they wished to target.

> Newspapers also give greater scope for more detailed comment and analysis of what are often complex and technical issues. A few groups actually expressed themselves wary of television publicity in case their views were over-simplified or distorted, though others saw in television an opportunity to popularise environmental concerns. (Lowe and Goyder, 1983, p74)

The current situation is vastly different, as the fifteen year gap has accentuated. There has been a complete reversal of media roles. Television is the medium which has supplanted newsprint in the environmentalists' favour. This argument is substantiated by the increased influx of television environmental documentaries e.g. Channel Four's Fragile Earth, Encounter and Nature series.

It is undeniable that the mass audience obtains a large proportion of its environmental education from the media. From within this brief historical context, it seems appropriate to give some consideration to previous and current research into the mass media and environmental issues.

Media research into environmental issues

The late 1980s have demonstrated an increase in media research on the environment. Research has been concerned primarily with the influence of the media on the audience and has concentrated on the extent to which viewers/readers rely on a mediated partial reality. Recent studies have focused on how the media construct meanings about the environment (Burgess, 1990, 1991; Love, 1990), the ways environmental groups devise strategies to challenge hegemony i.e. the ideological domination through the media (Cassidy, 1992), the relationship between the media and sources (Anderson, 1993), and the social construction of reality through the environment (Hansen, 1991). Research on the mass media and the environment has begun to move away from theories like structuralism, however, research approaches such as Marxism, semiotics and psychoanalysis still have validity in their application to the environment. Semiotics have been used to investigate issues such as oil spills e.g. identifying signs to reveal meanings manufactured by the media (Molotch and Lester, 1975). Similarly structuralism has been employed in studies (Fiske, 1987) attempting to define the extent to which the audience is influenced by the media.

Key authors who have written on the media's coverage of environmental issues include, Hansen (1990, 1991, 1993) whose work has compared television coverage of the environment in Denmark with Britain and Anderson (1993), whose research examines the relationship between the media and their sources. Burgess (1991) has carried out extensive studies into the ways landscape and conservation issues are mediated and the meanings which the media use to inform the public. Dunwoody (1984) has researched areas such as how science is mediated by journalists and reporters and their sources; in a study with Griffen (1993) she investigates coverage of risk situations, with reference to three contaminated sites in Wisconsin. Much has also been written on the ways in which environmental pressure groups harness the media to publicise their causes (Greenberg, 1985; Lowe, 1983, 1984).

Other important papers in this field range from general ideas about how the media covers the environment (Hansen, 1990) to specialised issues e.g. Sellafield nuclear power station and its effect on the community (MacGill, 1987); Chernobyl (Luke, 1987; Friedman, 1987; Rubin, 1987; Patterson, 1989), oil spills like Santa Barbara, Exxon Valdez and Braer, (Molotch and Lester, 1975; Wills and Warner, 1993; Davidson, 1990; Steinhart and Steinhart, 1972; Daley and O'Neill, 1991; Gundlach, 1977).

With this substantial increase in investigation into the media and environmental issues, it is evident that, a great deal of consideration has been given to the role of the press in dealing with the environment. Einseidel and Coughlan (1993) studied the construction of social reality by the Canadian press, investigating the meanings framed by the environmental news structure and the ideology which is conveyed through this. Hansen (1993) wrote about the press coverage of environmental issues with special reference to Greenpeace, in which he investigated a series of examples ranging from seal culling to nuclear power.

Where studies of the effects of environmental news coverage on the audience have taken place, methods such as content analysis have been employed. This research includes issues such as risk perception and analysis (Sandman 1988; Walters, 1989; Wilkins, 1987; and Burkhart, 1991, 1992). It must be pointed out, however, that these studies although, valuable in their contribution to the wider understanding of the mass media and environmental issues, are, for the majority, written from within a national or international context. To date there has been little written on the role of Scotland's media in the dissemination of environmental information to the social community. This work, therefore, attempts to identify journalistic source and information strategies and to ascertain to what extent the reporter objectively tries to formulate environmental news with a specific image of the audience in mind.

News and information

These terms are not synonymous, rather the latter is a metamorphic progression or evolution of the former. News and information are part of a process which is explained in detail in chapters 4-8.

What is news? Some definitions

News is, predictably, a concept which has been overdefined. It is almost impossible to find a new way of describing it in order to shed new light in a thoroughly researched area. However, it has been crucial to provide an explanation of "news" for the purposes of this work.

> [News is]...factual information that its viewers need in order to be able to participate in their society. (Fiske, 1987, p281)

Some journalists interviewed for this work defined news as follows:

> ...a news story is something that is a current event. A news story would be the fact that a report had been published that day or the day before highlighting higher pollution in the North Sea than they had seen or ever thought before. It would be, say, an announcement by the government that it was going to decommission half of the fishing fleet or it would be about oil spills or something...so it is about an event that has happened. A current event. [EC1(n)]

> News defines itself. What I see as news and what a newspaper editor sees as news are totally different things because we serve different areas and have different remits and so on. What I see as news is what I see that is of interest to the transmission area i.e. from Shetland...to Fife and out to the outer islands. It is a case of judging what is happening within the area at the time and trying to judge if that's important to the lives of people living within that area. [LNJ]

Three further definitions of news are put forward by Hall (1970), Ericson (1987) and Fowler (1991):

> ...the news is a product, a human construction, a staple of that system of "cultural production"...we call the mass media...the news is not a set of unrelated items; news stories are coded and classified; referred to their relevant contexts assigned to different (and differently graded) spaces in the media and ranked in terms of presentation, status and meaning. (Hall, 1970, p1056)

This is not a straightforward definition because it implies that the news media use interpretive measures to indicate which issues should have greater priority. Hall suggests that the system for choosing stories is subjective to those media, and that there is some measure of information control involved.

> News and other "information" are knowledge. They have been interpreted in context and given particular meanings. They may be given meanings as they are transformed and used in additional contexts as distinct from "information" in the original context. They are knowledge in all contexts in the sense of being given an objectivated, real meaning that is used in action and has social consequences. (Ericson, 1987, p11)

Ericson suggests that the information which exists originally is caused to change as it is interpreted and different meanings are placed on it. Original information exists but journalists add objective meanings which alter its information meaning structure. The metamorphosed information becomes "real" knowledge/information i.e. "real" in the sense that the information can be used to direct society. Therefore, it has real implications. These ideas have been drawn upon and referred to in this work and will be expanded on in later chapters.

Fowler (1991) defines news in this way:

> ...news is socially constructed. What events are reported is not a reflection of the intrinsic importance of these events, but reveals the operation and artificial set of criteria for selection. Then the news that has been selected is subject to processes of transformation as it is encoded for publication, the technical properties of the medium - television or news print for example and the ways in which they are used are strongly effective in this transformation. (Fowler, 1991, p2)

Fowler takes the ideas of Hall and Ericson further by suggesting that

8

not only is the order of news schedules unrelated to the significance of events due to meaningless news values referred to by media personnel, but that the information meanings are changed as senior journalists/editors review it and refine it for the broadcast or the press media. Implicit in these ideas are the issues of bias, and information interpretation but also it is suggested that the media play some subversive, manipulative perhaps even ideological role. The journalists, interviewed for this work, suggested that bias is an inherent part of the news process and cannot easily be avoided.

McQuail (1993) in his comprehensive review of objectivity cites news as,

> ...a continuing guide to and summary of recent or current events and items of immediately useful information. It is produced under strong pressure of events', under conditions of intense competition with other media, which have their own versions of the day's agenda and from which it is difficult for any one medium to stray. News has also to meet quite restricting 'product specifications' which are built into the news form and embedded in the normal expectations of audiences. (McQuail, 1992, p275)

News is new, fact based, a means of social education, of interest to society, therefore, applicable to people's lives. The majority of the audience is interested in issues which are closest to their own situations. Indeed some factions of the local audience view national news as unrealistic, far removed and a "window on the world but someone else's world" (Fiske, 1987, p289).

The definitions of the theorists Hall, Ericson, Fowler and McQuail are detailed and contain complex assumptions. These assumptions state that, firstly, news is a cultural product which is constructed in a particular way and that it is not a selection of unconnected issues which are chosen at random and ordered at will. Rather it is a product of a rigorous routine during which stories are judged against a set of standard criteria to assess their value or newsworthiness. They are then "ranked according to presentation, status and meaning" (Hall, 1970, p1056) i.e. news is structured according to a strict hierarchical order.

All the theorists agree that news is a product. However, McQuail (1993) indicates that, news is "useful information" and that it provides a "continuing guide to and summary of recent or current events" (p275). He states, as other theorists in the field do, that news must adhere to "strict specifications" which are part of the routine, but he also takes this further by saying that news is also confined by the "normal expectations of the audience". In other words, news cannot appear different either in terms of presentation or content because the audience would find it unacceptable.

Another important idea which has emerged is that the original information goes through a process of transformation as new information meanings are added. The knowledge which exists in a primary i.e. unmediated, complex and technical form becomes interpreted, simplified knowledge.

The theories of news appear within many different academic contexts e.g. social construction of reality, hegemonic reality, audience interpretation, information change etc. News is, therefore, a complex arrangement of information which has been constructed in a new way by journalists placing their own meanings (cultural and organisational) on it, and reflects an understanding or a perception of social reality.

The media as information seekers

The ideas of the media as providers of information or educators of the social community have been taken into account, but what about the flow of information from source to media? The ways in which journalists seek information and the sources they consult are vital parts of the information chain which links complex environmental issues with the audience or readership.

The role of the media library is a vital part of the journalist's information strand. Eagle (1992) edited a text on information sources for the media and it provides a unique insight into the relationship the journalist has with the library and emphasises the importance of the resource as a support facility.

A great deal has also been written on the media library as an information repository (Semonche, 1993; Arundale, 1986; Vergusson, 1985; Nev, 1988) and specifying Scotland (Heaney, 1986; Oppenheim, 1991). Related issues in the field include, the influence of electronic news sources on the news process (Neuwirth, 1988), and the application of technology to media libraries (Crowley, 1988).

There is a great deal of literature about how journalists seek their information, what information strategies they implement (Joseph, 1993; Hesketh, 1993; Nicholas, 1987a, 1987b; Gamage, 1993) and information management (Orna, 1990; Duncan, 1993; Arundale, 1991).

Koch (1991) provides an academic overview of the information dimension to news making by concentrating on the technology involved in its creation e.g. online databases and CD-ROM facilities. Other writers in this field include, Stanbridge (1992); Jacobson (1989); Briscoe and Wall (1992); Stover (1991); Levinton (1990); Ojala (1991); Leonard (1992); Arundale (1989).

It is evident, then, that there has been a substantial amount of interest in the areas of new technology and its application to the media library. However, it should be noted that this recent research has taken place generally at a national or international level, often using large newspaper organisations as case studies.

News construction and agenda setting

Hall, in his article, "The World at One with Itself" reminds us that news is a humanly constructed product. He states that news is not just information which spontaneously appears in a random order.

> Journalists and editors select from the mass of potential news items, the events which constitute "news" for any day... News selection, thus, rests on inferred knowledge about the audience, inferred assumptions about society and a professional code or ideology. (Hall, 1970, p1056)

Downs (1972) suggested that society in America was regulated by an "Issue Attention Cycle", where certain issues would come to the forefront of the social agenda, maintain this level for a period of time and then slip down the hierarchy and fade away.

> The cycle begins when, perhaps through a dramatic event, a piece of investigative journalism, or the revelations of a crusading individual, the general public is suddenly made aware of the existence and evils of particular problems which may well have been festering unnoticed for a considerable time. (Lowe and Goyder, 1983, p31)

Downs divides the cycle into five main stages, starting with what he calls the pre-problem stage. This is where a disagreeable social situation exists but it is unknown to the general public. It is at an expert level where specialists are aware of and disturbed by it. Stage two is the alarmed discovery and euphoric enthusiasm level where due to some dramatic events, the public is made aware of the problem and is alarmed by it. There is, at this stage the desire to have an instant solution to the problem. Realising the cost of significant progress is the next step, where the cost of the solution is extremely high. Gradual decline of intense public interest follows the other steps which Downs describes like this,

> as more and more people realize how difficult, and how costly to themselves, a solution to a problem would be, three reactions set in...discouraged...threatened...bored...And by this time, some other issue is usually entering Stage Two; so it exerts a more novel and thus more powerful claim upon public attention. (Downs, 1972, pp39-40).

The final stage, is the post problem stage. An issue which has been supplanted, moves off the agenda and remains as an issue of lesser concern (Downs, (1972); quoted in Hogwood, (1992), p1-2). Downs used this political theory and applied it to environmental issues which he thought were robust enough to stand up against the cycle. He believed that because of advantages such as the visibility of the environment; the fact that technology could combat environmental problems; that the costs involved need not necessarily be redeemed through taxation etc., environmental issues might be saved from their eventual demise more gradually (Hogwood, 1992, p2-3). Lowe and Goyder (1983), are in agreement with Downs' model but suggest that,

> ...other issues, like their predecessors, are not random and unconnected, but are part of a bundle of related concerns to do with material well being and physical security, concerns such as unemployment, inflation, Britain's industrial decline, social disorder, international tensions and the arms race. Moreover, rather than being caused simply by media fashions and the fickleness of public interest...these shifts in attention are related to changes in social values. (Lowe and Goyder, 1983, p32)

Hogwood (1992), rightly, asks the question "is there an issue attention cycle in Britain?" Interestingly, he concludes that the model does not apply to any of the political issues he tested.[1] Therefore, there is no evidence to suggest that there is not an issue attention cycle pertaining to environmental issues in Britain today. Further, it would seem reasonable to apply the five categories highlighted above, to environmental concerns. The Braer oil spill received world wide coverage at the time (Jan. 1993) and after extensive analysis of a local paper, it was noticed that the movement of the issue down the news agenda was fairly rapid. Only ten days after the incident, the story had been all but dropped from the newspaper and after only five days the issue had moved off the front page. Although this coverage is lengthy for a daily paper, this issue would seem to fit with Downs' model.

News values - News criteria

News values which govern the information gathering and story construction procedures are inherent in the news process. It is against this list of criteria that journalists measure the newsworthiness of an event and judge whether or not to include it. Hetherington (1985) developed a "seismic scale" of news values. This list included categories such as, "drama", "scandal", "proximity", "surprise" etc. It was against this scale, he suggested, that he was able to decide where to rank stories in the news hierarchy. Lowe and Goyder (1983) suggest that environmental issues, by their nature, are newsworthy, due to their aesthetic values.

> There is the strong emotive and moralistic appeal of issues which can be presented as a simple conflict of good versus evil. (Lowe and Goyder, 1983, p76)

Lowe and Goyder make the point, therefore, that one of the main reasons for media's fascination with environmental concerns is that these issues are not always political but are of human interest. However, the journalists, who were interviewed for this study, believed that the environment as a news story tends to appear lower in the news agenda because the issues are generally classed as long term problems which takes time to develop. It is the environmental disaster which takes precedence at the top of the news agenda.

Different newspapers have different news values and editors have different perceptions of news sense or news judgement. Patrick (1990), defines this as,

> ... the ability to assess a story in the light of the educational, social, political and cultural standing of the readers of his or her newspaper or magazine and in the context of any other interest the publication is designed to serve. (Patrick, 1990, no pages)

Musburger (1991) says that the news process is composed of various "mental stages", one of which is called "news judgement" or editorial control.

Final editorial control will lie with the news producer or news director. But each shot you [the videographer] frame and each sequence you shoot will require your making a judgement of its newsworthiness, its legal status and the part it will play in the assignment. (Musburger, 1991, p11)

In making a value judgement like this the journalist is implying a subjectivity on the information by adding his/her own interpretation and bringing his/her own cultural and social values to it. This would seem reasonable in light of the fact that information changes according to the ways in which it is selected and interpreted.

McQuail (1993), discusses news values within the context of the information industries. He believes that it is necessary to have realistic criteria to work to. Boyd (1993) in pitching his advice to journalism students, summarises news values thus,

> ...when a story has both proximity and relevance, the reaction it provokes in you will depend on your upbringing, environment, education, belief and morality. In other words, news values are subjective and for most news editors, the selection of news is more of an art than a science. Stories are weighed up by an instinctive process they would put down to news sense. (Boyd, 1993, p4)

He continues by saying,

> Every editor would agree that the greater the effects of a story on listeners' lives, their incomes and emotions, the more important that item will be. And every editor knows that if a news service is to win and hold an audience, the bulk of its stories must have impact on most of the people most of the time. (Boyd, 1993, p4)

News sense is an elusive concept which editors possess. It has been described by news people as being a kind of sixth sense which is instinctive and is acquired through experience. Fowler (1991) observes that news values are qualitative concepts that are not only connected with the selection of the information but also with the interpretation of items. In other words, an issue is only selected if it conforms to an established criterion within a certain context, thus indicating that selection via news values is an ideological process. Coote (1981) includes examples in her definition of news values. She talks about a hierarchy of values and indicates, also, that they are criteria which have been formulated for and by the patriarchy.

> We concur in decisions about what is a "good story" and what is not, what is central and what is peripheral, what is "hard" news and what is "soft"...These [news values] have been developed of course by white, middle class men, generation upon generation of them, forming opinions, imposing them, learning them and passing them as Holy Writ. We have inherited a hierarchy of news values. What are the major stories of the day?...A "hard" story is generally deemed to be one based on facts, on something precise which has happened in a particular sphere already labelled as "important". A story based on description, individual experience, nuance - a "human interest" story, perhaps; or something which has happened in a sphere not labelled "important" - may be considered good, but is nevertheless "soft" or "offbeat". (Coote, 1981 quoted in Hartley, 1982, p80)

Environmental news is very often covered from a human interest perspective, for example, the seal culling in Canada, the Braer oil spill in Shetland and the Exxon Valdez oil spill in Alaska. Environmental news is viewed by the audience and news practitioners alike as being "soft" because this type of reporting is so different from the "hard" journalism of crime or politics. But it is clear that environmental information is complex and technical, pluralistic and also multidisciplinary. It is often composed of "hard", scientific data and quantifiable as well as qualitative facts, therefore why does it receive apparent, "feminine" handling? "Feminine", that is in the sense that the facts are often "softened" with a human interest style format as opposed to the "masculine" approach to subjects such as crime or politics. For example, pictures of seals before and after the culling call up deep human emotions of anger, pity and sadness but this is not always balanced by an explanation of the environmental rationale behind this action.

Environmental "disasters" demand immediate media attention (Lowe and Goyder, 1983, p76). Sea disasters such as the Torrey Canyon which spilt 117,000 tons of crude oil when it crashed on the south west coast of England and the blow-out at the Union Oil Company platform in Santa Barbara, California in 1969, monopolised the media. Although there have been far more serious oil spills since then, these two examples remain the two most publicised incidents in environmental history (save perhaps for the Braer, Jan. 1993). Analysis of press coverage of the Exxon Valdez "disaster" (Daley and O'Neill, 1991) suggests similarities with coverage of the Braer. The widespread use of the word "disaster" at times early in the situation, when it was unclear as to whether it could be termed as so, was a major factor, as was the fact that initial coverage indicated themes of confusion, the underplaying of official reassurance and the victim role played out by the public (Daley and O'Neill, 1991, p45). These points would underline the features common to both "disasters".

Objectivity and bias

In his thorough, analytical review of the media, McQuail (1993) divides the issue of objectivity and bias into two parts, the Cognitive or Informational aspects and the Evaluative dimensions whereby the audience make value judgements about the world based on the information disseminated to them by the news media. He states that the standard of information quality against which news should be measured is based on the ability of the audience to formulate a concept of reality.

> The degree to which different observers might agree on the 'facts', the degree to which reports can be acted on with some confidence, the degree to which they are likely to prove consistent with personal experience. (McQuail, 1993, p124)

Tuchman (1972), rightly, suggests that in order to discuss objectivity comprehensively, three important factors have to be taken into consideration. These are "the news procedures as formal attributes of news stories and newspapers", "judgements based on interorganisational relationships" and "common sense used to assess news content" (p678). Her study concludes that there is no clear relationship between the aim (objectivity) and the method (news process) and that,

> objectivity refers to routine procedures which may be exemplified as formal attributes...and which protect the professional from mistakes and from his critics...the word objectivity is being used defensively as a strategic ritual. (Tuchman, 1972, p678)

Koch (1991) believes that news is not a set of impartial facts which have been linked together as part of a larger context, he maintains that news is someone's interpretation of an issue or concept. He states that today's journalism is unable to present the facts in an unbiased manner and that this is due, largely, to the media's information production and data retrieval techniques.

16

> For news to be "objective" it must treat all sources equally. To serve as an unbiased source of information, media outlets must be able consistently to describe events not as one or another specialist group wants them to be portrayed but rather in some way distanced from those partial, limited interpretations. (Koch, 1991, p5)

The media are implicitly involved in monitoring each other. Journalists do not tend to use paperbased sources of information to any great extent and, therefore, one of the primary sources is other media i.e. television news channels including satellite, daily newspapers and radio. Thus, in effect, there is a communal store of information which is drawn upon and upon which decisions for stories are made. Effectively the media, then, are information providers not only for the audience but also for themselves.

Fiske (1987) explains the positive objectivity critique by saying this,

> [Objectivity] plays an important role in the ideology of news and the reading relations that news attempts to set up with its audiences. The impossibility of objectivity and the irrelevance of notions of bias (based as they are upon an assumption that non-bias is possible) should be clear, but should not blind us to the ideological role that the concept of "objectivity" plays. (Fiske, 1987, p288)

Fiske states that objectivity is impossible to achieve due to the fact that the news process itself is subjective. Journalists through their retrieval of information, interviews with sources, construction of the news, place different meanings on the information causing its format to change and altering it so that it becomes, subjectively, an organised collection of facts. This suggests that the information is biased eg the Soviet coverage of Chernobyl was biased because the news information was selected by the government which had a hidden political agenda (Luke, 1987). "Bias" is a term often associated with negative views of the news process because it implies a subversive role which the media plays to influence the audience ideologically. According to McQuail (1993) and Fiske (1987), the bias which is implied in news reports is often unintentional and more often than not unavoidable. Fiske also says that, in his opinion, the notion of "objectivity" is an impossibility but the fact remains that news is ideological.

Ideology is the made up belief systems perpetuated by the dominant social power groups e.g. government.   Hartley (1982) argues that ideology is implicit in news discourse,

> implicit in this notion is the idea of the journalists/news relationship positioned between the two poles of "objectivity" (mediated) reality and the "subjective" (experienced) reality. This relationship determines what meanings will finally be produced. It follows that both poles have an influence in the "dialogic" production of meanings and that is relevant for ideological meanings as much as for any others. (Hartley, 1982, p142)

Therefore, Hartley is saying that the ideological meanings implicit in news text emerge as a mixture of the mediated and experienced concepts of reality. The journalist adds meanings to the issue due to the nature of the news process.

The alternative view to the positive objectivity critique is the belief that there is no such thing as objectivity (McNair, 1994), the idea is simply a mythical routine which has no validity. McNair agrees with Fiske (1987) when he starts his critique of objectivity by stating that "journalism is not and never can be a neutral, value free representation of reality" (p31). He agrees with many of the other theorists and academics (Hall, 1970; Fowler, 1991, Fiske, 1987) that news and the journalism profession are social constructions and that news is ideological and cannot, therefore, be value free (McNair, 1994). He also believes that news has to be about conflict which generates negativity because this is more newsworthy and newsworthiness is linked to economic and organisational considerations. McQuail states,

> unwitting bias is especially problematic because it is often embedded in the very practice of objective news reporting...Normal news collecting and processing routines and reliance on regular sources tend to influence selection in a systematic way.   Bias can also stem from the evaluative character of all languages and the unthinking deployment of wider interpretative frames and schemes for telling particular news stories. (McQuail, 1993, p190)

Bias exists, therefore, in journalism but it is not necessarily intentional. Rather, it is the consequence or symptom of the news process itself. For example, The Shetland Times had the difficult task of reporting on a major environmental issue which occurred on the island. Language is ideological and it is an element common to each discourse particularly news. Therefore, bias is unavoidable in the media. The social

18

constructionists' argument underlines this,

> ...journalism, regardless of the integrity of individual journalists and editors is always a selective, partial account of a reality which can never be known in its entirety by anyone. (McNair, 1994, p31)

The study of journalism, itself, as a profession, has always been founded on the fact that "..information was produced; selected, organised, structured and, therefore, biased" (Collins, 1990, p20).

> There is an enormous volume of potentially relevant information (requiring selection more than collection) which has to be processed under pressure of time. Sources may not readily supply information and there is often intense competition with other journalists for the same information. Information has also to be selected and presented to please consumers and to attract attention, thus emphasising form more than content. (McQuail, 1993, p185)

Boyd (1993) not only implies that the information is biased due to the process but also indicates and reinforces the idea that news is an extremely structured product which is assembled under the pressure of competition from other journalists and advertisers.

> Journalism...is often said to be our "window on the world", our means of contact with a world which, though shrinking is still largely beyond our direct personal experience. It provides the information from which we draw our "cognitive maps" of reality. (McNair, 1994, p18)

Theorists writing or studying in the field of the sociology of journalism (Fiske, 1987), frequently make reference to the "transparency fallacy" or the fact that news (particularly television news) acts as our "window on the world". Some academics believe that in fact news is not a window on the world, for this suggests some heightened sense of reality, when in fact, the media can only provide a simulation or interpretation of reality. The audience's ability to make sense of "our own personal environment and the world at large is through discourses which themselves have made us what we are" (Hartley, 1982, p141-2). Hence the ideological function discussed above. The ways we perceive our own local space, is by using what McNair (1994) calls our "cognitive maps" of reality. The idea of these "cognitive maps" was devised by Hall. We use these to construct our social reality i.e. what is real seeming to ourselves.

The primary aim of this work is not to discuss the cognitive processing abilities of the audience. An intellectual examination of cognitive mapping techniques is beyond the scope of this book. However an examination of the news at this level cannot omit a reference to the social construction of reality.

The social construction of reality

> Journalists as reporters of news are at the same time social actors, with a key role to play in shaping our perceptions of what news is and how to react to it. (McNair, 1994, p19)

News uses cultural maps to help the audience understand "the unusual, unexpected and unpredicted events which form the basic content of what is newsworthy" (Hall, 1978, p19).

Hartley (1982) states that implicit in these cultural maps (used by both journalists and the audience) are the beliefs that society is compartmentalised in similar ways to a newspaper e.g. sport, politics, crime etc. He calls this 'fragmentation' because the world is split up into a series of manageable chunks and is categorised by subjective themes. He says that journalists assume that the world is managed by and contains individual persons "who control their own destiny [and] therefore that actions are the result of their personal intentions, motives and choices" (p82). This negates the belief that social groups act and perform newsworthy responses or actions. The news also assumes that culture or society is ranked hierarchically in an order of importance. "Some people, events, spheres are more important than others. And the hierarchy is centralised both socially and regionally" (Hartley, 1982, p82).

The final important category which journalists take for granted is the idea of consensual reality:

> ...consensus requires the notion of unity: one nation, one people, one society, often translated into "ours", "our" industry, "our" economy, "our" nuclear deterrent, police force, balance of payments etc. within the notion of unity goes the notion of diversity, plurality, fragmentation. The different spheres of society interlock in institutions, organisations and personnel, each within the notion of fragmentation goes the notion of hierarchy, with all the spheres ranked in order of importance and all of course represented by their associated personalizations. (Hartley, 1982, p82)

Consensus, then, is the idea that society is united in its view of the national identity. The nation's role in international conflict is represented by a "them-and-us" situation which is constantly reinforced by the media's interpretations. The Braer coverage by Scottish newspapers tended to use this technique in an effort to imply an air of solidarity among the people of Shetland. Although taking note of the work which has been carried out into cultural and cognitive maps, this book does not seek to extend and develop these pyschological themes.

Another feasible hypothesis, explored by Cohen, is that the fiercer the competition between the media, the greater the desire to simplify the content in order to attract a larger audience (Cohen, 1990). Many of the subject specialists who were referred to by the press during the Braer incident are of the opinion that the intellectual content of some environmental issues is lost due to the fact that journalists reduce the concepts to the lowest point of comprehensibility, although, this is unavoidable in practical journalism,

> the job of a reporter is to render jargon and officialese meaningful to the lay reader. [LNJ]

However, news events are portrayed with less complexity than they are when they occur in real life. This reinforces Cohen's theory. Fiske (1987) explains how the reality factor works, by saying,

> realism does not just reproduce reality, it makes sense of it - the essence of realism is that it reproduces reality in such a form as to make it easily understandable. It does this by ensuring that all links and relationships between its elements are clear and logical, that the narrative follows the basic laws of cause and effect and that every element is there for the purpose of helping to make sense: nothing is extraneous or accidental. (Fiske, 1987, p24)

MacGuen and Coombs (1981) rightly suggest that there may be a case for supposing that individuals make decisions and judgements based on their own objective environments and not simply on the media's interpretations. However, they also point out that due to the concentrated nature of issues reported by the press, the audience experiences an image of reality. Due to the way news is selected, it is often biased towards negativity. It has been suggested that the way crime, for example, is covered, causes the reader or viewer to believe that the world is more violent than it really is.

21

Crime committed in the immediate neighborhood can be expected to give sufficient cause to provoke concern in the average citizen about self protection...Thus, while only fractions of the population are victims, we expect changes in the crime rate to bring the issue to the attention of entire neighborhoods and thus affect the aggregated national concern with law and order. (MacGuen and Coombs, 1981, p87)

How realistic is it to say, then, that environmental issues have a similar impact on the audience? Environmental news, particularly "disasters", is generally framed pessimistically and coverage is intense, thereby, reinforcing the negative images which surround issues. It may be likely, then, that the audience does indeed receive a picture of reality but whether this influences them negatively or misinforms them, is another matter and conclusions cannot be drawn without evidence from an effects study. The research of MacGuen and Coombs (1981) was not conclusive in this. They say,

the public clearly appears much more sensitive to the symbolic representations of public life than to any measure of the world they were actually experiencing. (p 88)

They do not say that the media's accounts of the environment, affects people in a negative or detrimental way.

A central component of this chapter has been to indicate and examine the relationship between the media and environmental issues. Viewed historically, it is evident that media research in the environment has only recently come to the forefront of communications studies. This may be in direct response to the heightened publicity of the environment, given by the media in the late 1980s.

The chapter has dwelt, at some length, on definitions and discussion of some of the theories put forward by media philosophers, using illustrations and examples of oil or sea "disasters". These included ideas such as news as a construction, the interpretation of information, and the metamorphosis of information meanings. Implicit in these ideas are issues such as the influence of the media on the audience or readership and the ideology conveyed through news.

It was suggested that Britain may have an issue-attention cycle as regards the environmental agenda, a topic which will be raised in a subsequent chapter.

An examination of news values and the news hierarchy was

included and linked to this was a detailed account of objectivity and bias, in which important themes such as self-examination by the media and the ideological implications of partiality are embedded. The final section referred to the social construction of reality. Ideas about fragmentation of the environment and the cognitive maps of reality which the audience uses to make sense of the world have been highlighted and developed.

The subject of the mass media and environmental issues has been introduced to set the scene in which we can examine how the media constructs this type of news in Scotland. The book aims to demonstrate how Scottish journalists gather information, which sources they use and what strategies they implement to reconstruct environmental issues for the wider social community.

Note

1. None of these were environmental issues.

2 News Construction Model

Introduction

Information is pluralistic, complex and technical. It is, therefore, represented in a number of different formats. This information changes as it is retrieved or gathered, packaged and disseminated (by journalists, librarians). Further, this information is influenced and redirected by the news process.

Journalists use "taken-for-granted" or tacit rules in the news process with which to gather information, construct and interpret the environmental information for news. The information is simplified by journalists for mass consumption. It is, thereby, reduced, condensed, distilled and repackaged as a different product.

A model was used to test these claims.

News construction model

The communication model was developed so that it could be tested in the field against information gathered from news personnel. It describes one of the main hypotheses which suggests that as environmental information is retrieved and interpreted by journalists, the meanings which can be taken from this information changes.

The model exists in a number of different stages and this chapter is concerned with describing the progression and revision of the research hypotheses in pictorial form. This section is divided into three parts, the preliminary, the secondary and the tertiary phases of the model.

The preliminary stage of the model is a flow chart diagram which shows the diverse levels of knowledge which are altered as a result of retrieval and interpretation. The layout appears to be abstract, but an explanation is included. The design is similar to that of the model produced by Ericson (1987) who demonstrated the selection/production sequence in two different media - newspapers and television.

The preliminary stage

The function of this stage of the model was to try and explain the flow of environmental information from sources to audience through the news process. The flow diagram represents a group of numbered concepts which interact with the flow of knowledge. The lines allow the reader to be taken through the various concepts.

General hypotheses reflected in model

Environmental information is changed as people e.g. journalists, librarians, the audience/readership interpret it. As environmental knowledge is retrieved and interpreted by journalists and news practitioners, the meanings which can be taken from this information diversify. It is suggested that information changes according to how it is used and interpreted.

It is also proposed that the flow of knowledge is influenced and redirected by the news process. Unmediated knowledge (unmediated by news media) ie information existing in environmental directories, academic works is altered into a popularised, commercial form and it appears to have been simplified due to the interpretive journalistic process (see tertiary stage). In a news report the information may still be complex but it has been shortened and reduced to a series of manageable concepts thus implying that some of the intellectual content of the original idea has been lost or changed i.e. that knowledge has been popularised.

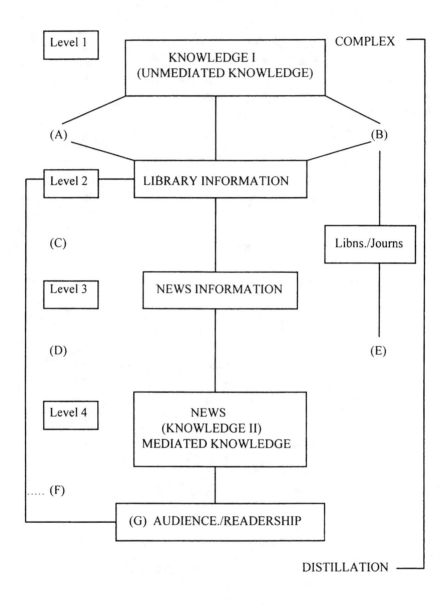

Figure 1 Mediation of Environmental Knowledge through the News Process (preliminary stage)

Knowledge exists on a number of different levels. KNOWLEDGE I represents the unmediated environmental information which exists in bibliographies and directories and is accessed by subject specialists or experts. However, experts modify or simplify this complex, technical information for journalists when they interact with them. This is the first level.

(A) The knowledge is retrieved and compiled by CD-ROM and on-line distributors e.g. ENVIROLINE; ENERGYLINE; POLLUTION ABSTRACTS; WATERNET etc. As this information is retrieved by these distributors and therefore, interpreted, the information changes and it is accessed by library staff in media libraries or sometimes directly by journalists themselves. Journalistic staff in Scotland now have on-line and internet access. At the time of this research,[1] however, Scottish journalists had little access to electronic sources of information and the national and international coverage accentuated this difference (Eagle, 1991; Koch, 1991; Gamage, 1993).

(B) Simultaneously the knowledge which is also created by specialists can be retrieved by experts or subject specialists who use the information in their work. Often it would be directly accessed by this group of academics but sometimes it will be retrieved through an intermediary e.g. the librarian. It may be directly retrieved by journalists at this level, but more often the journalist tends to approach the specialist who explains and, therefore, interprets the environmental science for the reporter as a lay person.

Level 2 is LIBRARY INFORMATION. A useful starting point for the journalist is the library where they can retrieve information directly or through the librarian. Online or internet searches may be conducted through the library.

(C) The information is retrieved by librarians and journalists. This information will become an integral part of the environmental news story. It is possible that journalists refer to colleagues' work at this stage either from cuttings or electronically. This point defines the important relationship between librarians and journalists.

Level 3 the NEWS INFORMATION represents the combination of information gathered from the library, electronic information hosts and information from contacts. This is the result of the information which was interpreted through selection at (C). This level describes the information selection and rejection patterns practised by librarians and journalists.

(D)   NEWS INFORMATION is interpreted by journalists at this point.   The interpretive rules are detailed by the tertiary stage of the model.   It is interpreted by the journalist and this is also constrained by editorial influences.   The product after this stage will be the news.

(E)   This part of the model depicts a period of interaction between journalists and experts.   A point of conference where final details can be checked before the news report is completed.

Level 4   the interpretation of NEWS INFORMATION   creates level 4 or NEWS.   This is the mediated information or KNOWLEDGE II which the audience/readership consumes.   This is the final dissemination point which creates an awareness within the social community.

(F)   Often NEWS copy is put back into the library as source materials for other journalists to use at another time.   This is an internal information cycle.   Information is diluted and distilled in that it is re-retrieved from the library by journalists to incorporate into news information.   The model argues that the information meanings change each time information is retrieved and interpreted.

(G)   The audience/readership or social community to whom the NEWS is being disseminated.   The research considered the audience not as an explicit, multi-faceted entity but as a collective body or mass which is defined by the perceptions of the journalist.   Therefore the model must reflect this fact.   The secondary stage of the model demonstrates that the journalist writes and practices the news process (preliminary stage of model) with perceptions of the implied audience in mind.   It, therefore, addresses the subject of the audience/readership only in so far as the audience plays an integral part in the process of news production.

KNOWLEDGE I   has changed four times and each time has had new information meanings placed on it.   This stage of the model represents the hypotheses at a general level.

The secondary stage of the model depicts the creation of the news story from the starting point i.e. the identification of an environmental issue, and follows the journalists through the news process. This entails the gathering of information from personal (human) sources and non-personal (library and electronic) sources, the interpretation of the event and the dissemination of the end product. At this level the model has been redefined and revised as new information has been added and the emphasis realigned from an information-specific focus to a professional-practice focus.

This stage of the model is again a flow diagram, which indicates pictorially the generation of the news story from the point of commencement i.e. where the ecological incident occurs and where reporters are dispatched to the scene of the action, through the gathering of information from sources and the news process to product dissemination to the audience. The straightforward design of the chart and the use of directional arrows enable the reader to understand the movement of news information.

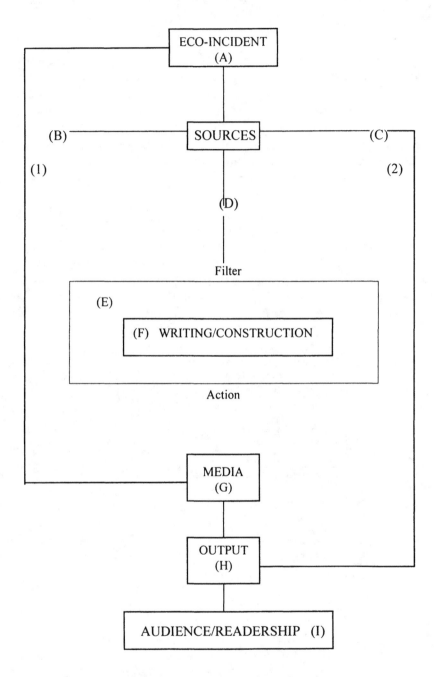

Figure 2 News Process Structure (secondary stage)

(A) The starting point at which the environmental "disaster" or incident, e.g. the Braer oil spill, takes place. Due to the sudden and unexpected nature of the impact of the event the issue is treated as extremely newsworthy by media practitioners i.e. news editors, and reporters are dispatched to the scene to gather information about the situation (route 1).

(B) Human Sources. Journalists rely on human contacts as opposed to paper-based or electronic sources of information. Reporters seek out and gather information about the issue by interviewing their own contacts in the area and experts or subject specialists from universities or research units. Journalists, also, contact emergency services (also identified by a number of authors in the field e.g. Hausman, 1992; Boyd, 1990) which help at the scene and can often reveal valuable information, due to the fact that they are the first to arrive at the incident. Local people (e.g. in the case of the Braer, the people of Shetland) and eye witnesses who were present as the event took place are interviewed for comment. Later (unless present at the time) reporters can contact environmental pressure groups, to get background information about the issues (primary and related) and to obtain a particular point of view about the incident. To counter this, very often, government sources are interviewed (in this case the local council, local and national government). These latter sources can be contacted through press conferences or information officers.

(C) These are "other" sources of information, e.g. libraries, which can hold large amounts of data for background material and other "disasters" against which parallels can be drawn and be used as examples (contextualisation). Media libraries are important information deposits and act as support facilities to journalists.

Of equal importance to some reporters are electronic sources of information e.g. CD-ROM, on-line databases and the internet. Recent evidence suggests that journalists can use information sources like *FT PROFILE* to check other newspapers, for example, *The Herald* uses this resource to search *The Scotsman* and vice versa. In addition to this most newspapers in the UK are now transferred onto CD-ROM or the internet e.g. *The Guardian*; *The Independent*; *The Scotsman*; *The Herald* which makes them easier to search more effectively.

(D) This is the story material which has been gathered at the three points above. It is preparatory material some of which will be used to write the article. This is a stage where information is selected or rejected and interpreted, therefore changed (see preliminary stage).

(E)   It is evident (see chapter 6) that, as journalists formulate the story they write with images of the audience in mind.   This is best described by the model as a filter action. The concept of the audience is at this stage an implied entity. Its image is that of an abstract concept which journalists perceive and aim to make explicit through their construction of news. Having gathered all the material at these other stages, journalists mentally target the audience/readership by selecting a level at which to package the environmental information. This image of the audience is reflected in the evaluative, operational, constructional/interpretive criteria implicit in the news process. Specifically, the evaluative criteria, for example, news values include details such as parochialism or the effort taken to ensure that news items are of interest and relevance to the news consumer.   The way also that language is selected at a level that the reader can understand and, in general, the comprehensiveness of the article as a whole are important constructional/interpretive features. This filter action which is implicit in the information strategies that the journalist has carried out, makes important assumptions about the audience for example that the audience is only able to "digest" or absorb a certain amount of technical information.

(F)   The News Process is described generally by the preliminary model stage. It demonstrates the different levels of knowledge which exist at each stage of the News Process from the complex and technical at the unmediated KNOWLEDGE I to the apparent simplification of environmental information at the dissemination stage. At this secondary model stage, the writing process, which is implicit within the construction process, exists only within the context of this specific filter action. This process is critical to the understanding of the audience as an implied entity.

(G) The media monitor each other constantly, in order to keep up to date with events as they happen (also identified by Ericson, 1987; Hausman, 1992).   Print media refer to broadcast news throughout the day and in the event of a "disaster" occurring can "hold" the front page or space within the paper to accommodate it. Similarly broadcast media routinely survey every daily newspaper to check up on facts and story angles.   Effectively there is a recycling of information due to this continuous referral process which occurs.   In the north east of Scotland, the daily and evening newspapers, *The Press and Journal* and *The Evening Express* monitor the television (BBC and Grampian Television) and radio (Northsound) output all day and vice versa.

(H) This stage in the model refers to the output or the finished news product which is disseminated to the audience via newspaper, television or radio.   After transmission or newspaper production, the output is collected and sent to the library where video tapes or newspapers are filed by subject. Often newspapers are not kept in their entirety but are cut up into important, relevant articles. These articles are now being transcribed onto microfilm, microfiche and CD-ROM. Old output is collated in the central deposit of the library for future reference where journalists can access it for other stories. This is essentially, again, a "recycling" of information whereby other journalists' work is referred to (see route 2).

(I) The model shows this as another point of interaction with the audience. However, at this stage the audience exists as an explicit entity. This is the multi-faceted, collective body that consumes the news product, becomes aware of the environmental issues which affects them and that accepts or rejects the interpreted information which has been disseminated directly to them. The research does not focus on the audience as a mass entity in order to ascertain what effects the news product has on it but aims to discover the audience through the perceptions and understanding that the journalist has.

Collectively, each stage of the model provides a unified overview of journalistic practice and complements the others in achieving a sense of understanding about the news process. The stages have evolved from the general to the specific, beginning with a macro (information perspective) level view of the news process. There follows a view of the news process structure (i.e. the application of the model to a specific, practical setting). The chapter is concluded with a general examination of the tertiary level of the model which demonstrates the interaction of the different rule categories implicit in the news process. The tertiary stage is discussed in full in chapters 4-8.

This stage of the model has been built on the strength of the evidence gathered from journalists and indicates specifically how environmental issues are evaluated, how information is gathered, how the news product is constructed and its meanings structured by journalists. It seeks to complete the news process model, providing a comprehensive explanation of the inter-related factors which constitute the rules used by reporters. The preliminary stage demonstrates the differing levels or states of knowledge which metamorphose as a result of information retrieval and reinterpretation. The secondary stage exists in parallel with this but at this specific secondary level it is contextualised by the addition of the hypothetical reporting situation. Essentially, the secondary stage indicates the movement and the mechanics of the news process when applied to a specific type of environmental coverage i.e. "disaster". It depicts, on a general level, some of the routine work practices which journalists carry out.

The tertiary stage is a detailed analysis of the news process and conveys an account of the rules which journalists use from an integrationalist perspective. It has been argued that journalists implement the news process through the execution of a number of different routine procedures. The research has identified the fact that there are taken-for-granted rules which govern the ways in which journalists carry out the news process. The construction of news is routinised by the repetition of the same sequence of rules and consequently, journalists perform them tacitly.

It became evident that the rule categories used by journalists are often used in combinations and influence each other i.e. they are not mutually exclusive. For example, the constructional and interpretive categories are both always used together as they are primarily concerned with the writing of the story. Therefore, despite the fact that the third category on the tertiary model is termed as constructional, it is implicit that this will include also the interpretive rules.

Note

1. The model was designed at a time when the impact of internet technology was not particularly advanced. See Nicholas [et al] (1997) for implications of internet on journalists' information gathering.

3 Subject Specialists

The media use a wide and varied range of information sources during the implementation of their information strategies (see chapter 7). Further, journalists have a preference for using human sources of information rather than paper-based ones. Therefore, it seems appropriate to look at the scientific subject specialist as vital point of reference for the journalist and to study this important relationship.

> ...The 1980s began with a public more wary of science and scientists than a generation before. The decade ended with mediated images of Challenger, Chernobyl and the Greenhouse effect as reminders that wariness is warranted. The shift had been years in the making. When the enemies were disease and hunger, science was an ally. When the enemy became overpopulation and pollution, science was a part of the problem as well as the solution. (Wilkins and Patterson, 1991, p197)

Academics like Wilkins and Patterson (1991) have observed that the audience or readership has changed its perceptions of the environment from ones of passivity to those of active involvement. They have also suggested that the media has altered its outlook on these types of issues. They continue,

> journalists began this century attempting to popularise science. Today they are more skeptical. Progress is no longer assumed when the news story is one of scientific discovery, nor is progress any longer always assumed to be desirable. (Wilkins and Patterson, 1991, p198)

The media popularise science but it is purported that this is rather more due to the nature of the news process itself rather than popularisation for the sake of it (see chapter 8). Wilkins and Patterson (1991) are right not only in observing a more sophisticated media attitude but also in suggesting that people are no longer surprised by scientific discovery and appear to be less challenged by scientific advancement.

Wilkins and Patterson (1991) make the following points. Firstly, the audience's faith in the media is paramount for the media's survival. Secondly, the audience is wary of science. This may be due to media interpretations (Nelkin, 1987, 1991; Wilkins and Patterson, 1991; Burkhart, 1987). Equally, scientists desire to communicate the correct knowledge at a suitable level for comprehension by the audience. The main way they do this is through the media. Thirdly, the media's relationship with scientists is undiscerning and journalists are often uncritical of specialists due to their lack of subject knowledge. This relationship is double-edged. Scientists are frequently distrustful of the media due to issues such as misquoting, misrepresentation and the wrongful interpretation of facts. However, the media feel the need to refer to scientists in order to validate news reports and the use of experts aids the credability factor.

The following points are examined below and the discussion draws on evidence gathered from a series of interviews with scientists (see List of Abbreviations).

1. The specialist reflecting on him or herself i.e. self-perception. How he or she envisages the self as the personification of knowledge.

2. The investigation of the relationship between specialists and journalists and in particular the specialists' perception of this relationship.

3. How specialists impart environmental information to the audience via the journalistic process i.e. how specialist information is changed by journalistic simplification.

Specialist self-perception

Scientists seem to adopt an educational role when dealing with the media. Indeed, the scientists were in favour of speaking to the press or broadcast media in order to educate the audience or readership in environmental matters. Many acknowledged that it was helpful to use the media as a vehicle of communication for scientific comment and to avoid conjecture. The consensus of opinion was that scientists should reply to journalists' questions openly and made the recommendation that a training course for scientists in ways to handle the press would be useful.

Scientists are very truthful but there is a naiveté in the way they answer the press. [A]

Other views of self-perception also emerged. Just as the journalists' self-assessment revealed that they have roles of social responsibility (see chapter 4), it was discovered that specialists fulfil roles of authority and authenticity. Scientists recognised their roles as influential in so far as they possess a specific knowledge of a particular academic area and that they communicate it to the social community via the media. Furthermore, they noticed that their views were used to authenticate information i.e. establish the truth or validate issues, a task which few others could accomplish. Scientists seem to have a very clear idea of their role when interacting with the media.

The relationship between the specialist and the journalist

Contact between the media and subject specialists is quite frequent. The scientists admitted that both the broadcast and print journalists contact them in a crisis situation if it happens to correspond to their area of expertise, although one of the specialists qualified her statement by saying that the local media will not usually approach her for advice, only for information which will provide publicity. The model shows experts at point (B) being approached by the media for information about the eco-incident (see secondary stage of model, chapter 2).

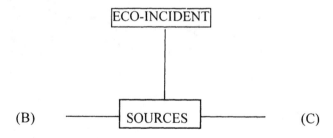

Figure 3 Excerpt from Secondary Stage of Model

Most universities have a central list of contacts within the institution and the press officer can put the press in touch with anyone whose expertise may be relevant. It would seem that there are two types of contacts list which exist. The first one is a list of specialists, owned and referred to by journalists. The second one is a list owned by the university or academic institution from which names are selected for the media if it is deemed appropriate by that institution. The scientists who were interviewed did not know of being on a list of contacts owned and used by the media.

Specialists apparently approach tabloid and broadsheet journalists differently. It was implied that tabloid papers have a tendency to misrepresent scientists more often than broadsheets. It is felt that the popular press is unable to handle complex information. One scientist felt apprehensive about speaking to journalists because of the danger of being mis-reported. It was suggested that there is a lack of even reporting in science subjects. In response to this problem, the Scottish Agricultural College, for example, sometimes use a system of prepared quotes. One scientist argued that there are no controls in an interview situation and, therefore, he prefers to write down the information and fax it through to journalists.

> It is important for specialists to represent their organisations properly and inaccurate reporting is seldom acceptable. [C]

The scientists felt that journalists are often forced to find a dramatic story to attract the attention of the audience or readership e.g. the Braer oil spill attracted media attention for weeks (see Figure 3, above). The specialists agreed that the long-term impact of these stories is barely newsworthy (in their opinion and this will differ from a journalists perspective, see chapter 6) although this does depend on the paper or programme covering the issue.

> TV - the later broadcasts are much more factual but the earlier programmes condense the information to give a particular view rather than covering all the angles. [A]

Before an interview, the scientists preferred to find out the angle that the journalist is going to take.

At the Braer [press] conference there was a wide range of specialist practitioners. One journalist wanted to know the chemical formulae of dispersants so that he could write about the toxic effects. Another person wanted to know how many oiled seals there were, so that he could take heart rending pictures. [C]

Specialists' mediation to audience/readership via journalists

The scientists felt that there is always a danger of the public becoming confused due to the fact that the audience varies in terms of comprehension ability and that the news is an interpretation of knowledge or the primary unmediated information (see Figure 1).

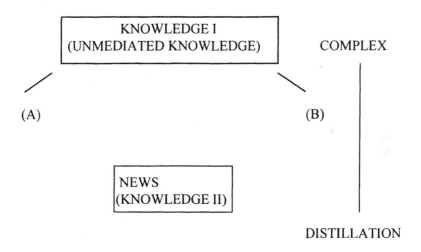

Figure 4 Excerpt from Preliminary Stage of Model

Two strands of opinion emerged from this part of the discussion. These were, firstly, that the information which is to be communicated is complex and secondly that this information is disseminated rapidly. The scientists felt that there should be more specialists who could communicate information to laypersons. One specialist said that this danger comes from the pressure on the journalist to condense what is said and that sometimes things cannot be reduced without losing their meaning. This substantiates the preliminary stage of the model (see chapter 2) which suggests that information meanings are altered, when information is retrieved, interpreted and mediated (see Figure 4). The model argues that the news product is altered information that has been interpreted by journalists using information that has been simplified by specialists (B). With a fast breaking story or one that has to have constant coverage, the information has to be gathered and assembled and the news mediated quickly to keep the audience/readership up to date. Although the audience might be confused by complex information, it is very dangerous to over-simplify an issue because the intellectuality of the idea will be lost.

> People will switch off or stop reading anything that is pitched on too high a level. [D]

> People are selective about information. [B]

Two separate themes emerged. Firstly, that people "switch off"[1] because they don't understand and secondly, that people are selective about information i.e. they "switch off" because they have received enough information or the particular information they wanted and do not need any more. Without studying the audience it is impossible to draw any firm conclusions. However, from the specialists' data, it appears that there are two different audiences which they are aware of or perhaps two different facets of the same audience: one which makes its own decisions and controls the flow of knowledge from specialist to self and another which finds it more difficult to amass the information and understand it. It can be argued, therefore, that the experts see part of their role as an educator. It is interesting that specialists perceive the audience in two parts because this is bound to have implications for the types of information offered to the media by specialists. The simplification process which specialists or experts carry out i.e. the selection and rejection of information and the reinterpretation of this information, causes the meanings attached to this information to change (as suggested by the preliminary stage of the model). The information metamorphososes more than once as it is retrieved and interpreted by specialists for mediation to journalists and then as journalists reduce the concepts for dissemination to the audience. By giving the scientist a briefing on the approach they want, journalists can help educate the specialist as to the level at which the information should be pitched.

Due to the complicated nature of the environmental field and the ways in which the media have handled it, the audience/readership now distrusts scientific subjects.

> Environmental issues require a wide field as it is necessary to balance interactive features. The width makes it confusing and complicates the thing. Despite the public's interest in environmental issues there are still many unbalanced views. The reason for the extremism in this field is unevenness of opinion. Over the last ten years, there has been a loss of trust in science by the general public. Part of this can be laid at the door of the media. [C]

Most of the scientists believed that generally news and documentaries portray environmental issues in a scientifically sound manner, although they were unanimous in saying that not all programmes were thorough in their research. The scientists identified quality broadsheets and television documentaries as being the most comprehensive. This implies that the scientists had less faith in television news bulletins which is due, perhaps, to the brevity and lack of depth with which items are mediated. It can be argued that this is due to the pragmatics of the process and does not seem to be intentional on the part of the journalist (see chapters 6, 7 and 8).

The information can be complicated for journalists and also for the audience to understand. Specialists break down this information into an intelligible format that simplifies the concepts. Some of the scientists, interviewed, indicated that they always pitch the information at a level reporters will understand by trying to highlight areas the public will be interested in. In doing this the journalists or the public can find out more information themselves. The specialist, therefore, has to change the information to make it more accessible for the public. The scientists felt that the media have a "don't-be-scientific-or-technical" attitude but this does not prevent them giving journalists information that is still pitched at a complex level. Therefore, journalists are receiving a mediated or interpreted form of the information.

There does not seem to be a formal structure to the relationship between the media (broadcast and print) and specialists. Experts are contacted when the need arises e.g. a crisis situation - the Braer oil spill. From the journalistic point of view, it is a case of building up a private list of contacts through experience (see chapter 7).

41

It is apparent that specialists see themselves as informing the public about a particular area of expertise. However, sometimes it is felt that the media may "manipulate"[1] the information, thereby altering its state and changing what needs to be communicated.

It is understood that interviewing specialists for their opinions and explanations of issues lends validity and authority to newspaper articles and often heightens the credibility of a journalist's profile. Ford Burkhart quotes Sarah Friedman in his paper "Media Functions and Environmental Management",

> if journalists' education is deficient in areas that might prepare them to understand and communicate the technical nature of risk and hazards, then some media advocates would argue that their obligation is to act as a surrogate for the layman, to absorb and transform technical information provided by either experts or mediators between experts and laymen and to relay that information to a public that often is even less well prepared to grasp technical information and concepts. (Friedman in Burkhart, 1992, p 77).

Journalists have to and should act as mediators between the scientists and the general public but specialists feel that often the information and its context is changed due to this simplification process (see Figure 1).

> ...Most people understand science and technology less through direct experience than through the filter of journalism. (Nelkin in Moore, 1989, p54)

Scientists try to accommodate the media by breaking down the complexities of a variety of scientific issues into straightforward language and relating it to the readers within a particular context. This type of information should be clearly defined without simplifying it or presenting it in a patronising and condescending manner.

The scientists talked with great emphasis about the effects of the news on the audience and also, about issues such as mis-representation, the mis-informing of the public and mis-reporting. However, this work does not have any of the above elements as its focus and, therefore, can address them only on a superficial and peripheral level.

Journalists' perceptions of subject specialists

Despite the argument that experts or scientists do not respect or regard journalists highly and vice versa, experts are definitely referred to as one of the most important sources of information in the reporting of environmental news (see chapters 7 and 8).

Groups of scientists and journalists were interviewed separately and clearly neither professional group perceived the other favourably. It has already been noted in this chapter that scientists believe journalists mis-represent and mis-report complex, scientific and environmental information.

Without having studied the subject specialist in greater detail, it is difficult to reach conclusions about their perceptions of the audience. However, both the experts and the journalists hold the common view that the audience should receive environmental information in its simplist form.

All the journalists, interviewed, admitted that they referred to experts or subject specialists in order to back up an environmental story. (For List of Abbreviations)

> We do use experts, local people, scientists, agriculturalists. We use the relevant people for the right story, though we don't have a list and use some over again. [1]

> We do use experts here. We have a good science correspondent and he has lists of contacts who can help. I do use contacts whose names I would never reveal. I protect my sources. They can be for example in Government Departments and it is to their advantage that they give the right information. [3]

When questioned as to why the media use experts, the journalists agreed that it was to substantiate or validate their stories.

> ...We are not experts ourselves. The organisation has specialists who can be consulted. Experts are fine if they can explain. [1]

Many of the journalists criticised the scientists for using technical jargon to explain complicated environmental concepts, which they [journalists] had to synthesise for the audience or readership. A self-comprehension test is applied to the information i.e. when the journalist understands the concepts, then the audience will also understand them.

If I don't understand it then the viewer isn't going to either. Television relies on visual aids constantly to help the understanding process. We let the pictures tell the story. We need to use maps and diagrams, for example, how an oil platform works. Graphics are sophisticated ways of breaking down complicated information and making it more visual. Television reinforces the information by using artwork, graphics, maps and diagrams. Viewers hear and see what is happening. The comprehension of viewers is enhanced. [3]

The journalists were adamant that there is a danger of the audience becoming confused by the issues which specialists discuss, unless the information is presented at the appropriate level for the audience to handle. This level is selected through the operational rules implicit in the news process (see chapter 7).

Don't underestimate the audience. They are selective about what they pick up. But if we [the journalists] don't understand then the audience won't either. There are ways of making the information more palatable. [3]

What this brief chapter has attempted to do is to draw out the theme of the subject specialist or expert as an information source for the journalist which is described by the preliminary and secondary stages of the model. It is undeniable that in the reportage of environmental issues, the scientist is one of the most important sources and, therefore, it seemed appropriate to capture a flavour of the unique relationship that exists between the two professional groups. The chapter has also tried to demonstrate the influence of the news process on the information flow from originating i.e. primary, unmediated source to the information consumers i.e. the social community.

The next chapter begins to look, in more detail, at the news process and the rules which journalists apply to construct the product we consume.

Note

1. This term was used by some of the specialists who were interviewed.

4 The Journalistic Rules for Constructing News

Journalists and news practitioners use taken-for-granted procedures which are regarded within the profession as being instinctive. The journalists, who were interviewed, found it difficult to rationalise the news process (findings which support White's (1964) work into wire editor's gatekeeping rules). March and Simon (1958) discovered that personnel in organisations routinised their tasks because this process of routinisation facilitated the control of work, a view echoed by Tuchman in the 1960s and 1970s. Tuchman's work argued that routinisation was impeded by a variability in raw material which was partially alleviated by a classification of news stories which news people carried out.

> Newsmen categorise events not only as happenings in the everyday world, but also as potentially newsworthy materials - as the raw material to be processed by news organisations. (Tuchman, 1973, p111)

Evidence from my research indicates that journalists do use tacit, routine procedures to construct the news i.e. research and compile stories, and "rules" have been inferred from these procedures. These "rules" were aggregated into groupings in order to better understand the types of procedures used in the news process. The "rules" were then assigned to particular categories and were labelled Evaluative; Operational; Constructional/Interpretive; and Editorial. Further, it was discovered that the rules used by journalists are often used in combinations when carrying out tasks. The categories are not mutually exclusive.

If the news process could be described chronologically, the execution of the different sets or categories of rules would be ordered in this way - evaluative, operational, constructional/interpretive, with the editorial ones being applied actively throughout. The tertiary stage of the model explains that news practitioners use their news sense (or evaluative rules) to identify the newsworthiness of potential stories but subsequently write the article (constructional and interpretive rules) by targeting the issue appropriately for the readership.

The sources of the rules

> Firstly, journalists must be able to understand and interpret the social events with which they are confronted, and secondly, they must have the specific skills necessary to convey this information to their audiences. (Gaunt, 1990, p37)

The study showed that journalists routinise their work procedures and that they apply these rules tacitly to the news process. Where do these rules come from?

Two possible sources from which the rules might emanate could be training and on-site experience (i.e. the knowledge acquired on the job by osmosis and through trial and error). In order to investigate this the journalists were asked a series of open-ended questions. These questions unsettled them because the interview forced them to account for knowledge which they take for granted. Consequently, some journalists found this very difficult to answer and put it down to experience but could not elaborate, indicating something of the tacit nature of the process. In spite of these difficulties, a number of origins have been revealed by journalists and these have been categorised into themes. These are training; experience; editorial and organisational policy; professional role/self-image.

Training

The sample of journalists came from a wide range of educational backgrounds and it is evident that there are differences between the ways in which journalism students are trained today and the methods used fifteen to twenty or more years ago. Many of the senior members of the sample drew contrasts between the training then and now, as the following example shows,

> I think that young journalists now because of the nature of the business are thrown into the deep end and I think they are out an awful lot...But that's the changing nature of the job. I went out with...them [experienced journalists] as a kind of legman and they told you what to do and you learned by that. If someone tells you once in a forceful way [not to do something], you don't do it again, whereas they [novice journalists] do it

now and it gets in the paper and they think it's all right. Also they don't have the techniques [now] that reporters had - like the ways to approach people - where you persuade them. You pick things up without being aware that you're doing it. [NNJ]

Journalism education has been the subject of considerable research (Becker, 1988; Marsh, 1973; Gaunt, 1991; Luter, 1983). For example, Marsh's (1973) study of student teachers demonstrates that educators have a great deal of influence over their students.

Many of the journalists who were formally trained by journalism educators i.e. at undergraduate, post graduate or certificate level stated that they were dissatisfied with the ways they were trained. It was suggested that journalists have to "unlearn" concepts which they have been taught when they start working at a newspaper or broadcast institution.

It's not the sort of job where training makes a great deal of difference...Experience is everything and until you've done it there's not a lot anyone can tell you. You're self-motivated, self-taught and self starting.... [LNJ]

In Britain, the National Council For the Training of Journalists is the main training institution and most journalists (certainly the majority of the respondents in the sample) hold the certificate from NCTJ courses. The Council aims to train students in the recognition and selection of newsworthy facts from both written and verbal documentation; to write clearly balanced reports and to gain knowledge of the newspapers' departments and the industry's infrastructure (NCTJ cited in Gaunt, 1990, p45). In every course the emphasis is on the pragmatics of the news process and this is the reason (according to Gaunt) that British journalism is regarded as a craft rather than a profession.

Today, almost all training is given either in colleges of further education or on the job. The focus is on practical reporting not theory (Gaunt, 1990, p39). It is the practical side of training i.e. the on-site training which the journalists referred to most frequently. These college courses were classed by them as being academic.

What became clear during the course of the discussion about training was that the journalists perceived that there are fundamental differences between an academic and practically based learning experience. Training, it was suggested, is idealistic and divorced from the reality of the newsroom. On graduate courses, writing assignments are designed around a fictional village and reporters are taught to write in a non-biased, balanced way. Some of the journalists referred to this exercise and emphasised how artificial it is. They underlined the fact that the theory of objectivity does not exist in practical newspaper reporting and that forcing students to write using a technique which is not grounded in the pragmatics of the news process, prohibits them from quickly adapting to conventional newsroom practice when they assume a journalistic position.

The journalists were asked about the differences between their training and their job,

> ... that is a failing of the body that trained me - the NCTJ. It exists in this kind of a vacuum which never really existed. They construct this little village called Oxtown and everything happens in Oxtown and it is completely fictional. It's got a district council and a regional council, a court and a river and a school - everything you are going to need if you're going to write for a local paper. The way they make you write when you're training is completely different to what...well my experience anyway. It's false you know. If there was an Oxtown Gazette which is the paper that you are supposedly writing for...it would be the dullest paper in the world because they do impose all these ideals on you. You can't put emphasis on any particular area of the story. You have to be completely balanced , you have to be non-sensationalist, and it really is an unrealistic situation. [LNJ]

> I went straight from school so I suppose that I think that's the best way to do it...[the] journalism course is artificial and it's still a false environment. It's not really in the real world. [LNA2]

The majority of the journalists in the sample, received instruction from senior colleagues when they started work. In light of this evidence, it may be that in many cases new reporters did not learn these rules overtly i.e. learning by being told but rather by osmosis i.e. learning through the subtle, unconscious influence of others. Journalists often watched their colleagues and learned by example.

> I mixed with the journalists and saw how they operated and picked things up. I think it is very difficult to work on your own...I think you do need help. I think as you go along there are always people you look up to...one particular person who you think is good and you watch how he writes and that person will change as the years go by. [LNA2]

I received a great deal of help from journalists because you have to rely on them. This is not the sort of job that you walk into and pick up straight away. There is a definite learning curve and if there is not that curve then people are liable to fall flat on their faces. [LTJ]

I got some help but a lot of it is just listening to what people are doing. Just trying to pick up on what is happening. [NNJ]

Learning by osmosis means that journalists absorb the techniques which they must use to evaluate, operate and construct the news. It is after this process and through the repetition of the same routines that the knowledge becomes tacit i.e. inherent in the working practices of the journalist. Reporters, then, define the source of their rules as "experience".

Experience

This was a typical response to the probing questions about how journalists know what they know and about how they learn how to practice the news process. For example, one journalist replied that it was "basic experience" which he had acquired over a set period of time and thus enabled him to write stories for both tabloid and broadsheet simultaneously. When prompted further about whether this was learnt on the job or from a formal qualification, he replied,

I joined the paper straight from school and I was trained on a block release course. It was very, very basic but you do learn the fundamentals of reporting and they stay with you right through. But you learn through experience how to write. There are certain ways to pitch stories or certain issues. It is experience - there is no other secret about it. [LNA2]

Although the term "experience" was used constantly by respondents, they were unable to clearly define exactly what it consisted of or what it meant.

It is experience. You receive a basic training at college which sets rough parameters. But after a few years it becomes formulaic. If you have a story you must have an opposing view point...so there are certain rules that you use. It's a flexible pattern. It's instinctive but it's coached by your previous experience. Anyone can do it. It's pretty much common sense. [ENJ]

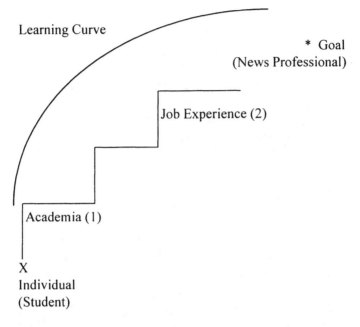

Figure 5 is illustrated with the following labels:

Learning Curve

* Goal
(News Professional)

Job Experience (2)

Academia (1)

X
Individual
(Student)

1) Academic practical - secondary experience
2) Experiential practical - primary experience

Figure 5 Different Routes to Journalism Experience

According to the journalists, the student starts initially with a basic instinct for news. This instinct is apparently more than a deep seated interest in the subject. It was described by the journalists as a naturally occurring intuition with which they can firstly identify what is newsworthy and secondly assess how to organise, interpret and disseminate the product. This apparent innate reaction is cultivated and extended only after the student starts to re-learn the news process in a practical, editorial setting. Those, who had completed graduate studies in journalism felt that a period of readjustment had to be endured after they started work. They had to cross a division that separates academic training from on-site experience. These two types of learning are defined differently. Academia, although professing to be practically led exists on a separate experiential level from on-site experience. This is because the training conveyed to students through academic courses is secondary i.e. it is communicated through an intermediary e.g. an educator or practitioner, or from within a specifically defined context e.g. training exercise or the simulation of a newsroom. Experience from an on-site position is distinct from this, in that it is primary and trainees learn in the real situation. The differences between academic training and "real life" work experience were so defined, that the journalists felt that they had to "start again" and re-educate themselves according to the news work patterns or routines.

Figure 5 also represents the fact that the student/practitioner is on a learning curve with the ultimate goal being the transition to news professional which is defined by organisational culture and personal values. Both journalism students (i.e. academic trainees) and journalism trainees (i.e. on-site trainees) recognise distinctions in the different methods of education.

This on-site experience (i.e. experience gained in a practical setting) facilitates the routinisation process because through the constant repetition of the rules, the same formulae become reinforced and journalists ultimately perform them tacitly.

> ...We're talking this through and I'm rationalising it but just purely from an operational point of view, when I'm working if I picked up a news release, I wouldn't be thinking right who's making the claims, right it is an environmental group...I'd just do it.....[I'd be aware] that they've got an axe to grind, they've got an agenda that they're working to, so I've got to be careful of this one. [LNJ]

> I don't really think about it. There's a trainee spending some time with us at the office and I can't explain what I do to him. I don't actually think about how I do it. I just kind of do it. I don't sit down and think about it - maybe I should think why am I doing this? [NNJ]

This journalist is a clear example of how the routinisation process and instinctive journalistic qualities have all combined and over an extended length of time, become ingrained into the working practices of the journalist. He carries out the news process without having to think or rationalise why he is doing it in a certain way. Moreover, he cannot communicate why he is doing it in this way.

It's on-site experience. On the job. It's really just experience. You just
go out there and do it. [NNJ]

It comes through experience. I've been doing radio for six years and
journalism for eleven. It just comes through experience. [LRJ]

Learning on-site, then, involves learning not only by osmosis but
also by trial and error. The mistakes made by new reporters are used as
educational devices. Each one is logged and a mental note is made not to
repeat it in the future, while at the same time, other rules are continuously
reinforced, thereby extending the learning process. Through these
experiences, recipe knowledge (Berger and Luckmann, 1967) is
advanced.

Journalism is a profession that involves a continuous learning curve.
Each journalist strives towards a professional goal and this is defined by
both the organisation and the self (see Figure 5). The familiarity with
issues results from experience. This experience manifests itself either in
the form of becoming a specialist reporter or an editor who has built up an
experiential code for the selection and rejection of issues. Personnel who
have worked at the paper or organisation for a length of time, can often
second guess editors because they have acquired a clear insight into the
policies, news values and requirements of the institution.

[I know how to do this] from having worked on the paper for so long. I
can tell you what the reaction of my boss would be if I took this story to
him and said, "look what do you think of this?". He would say, "yes fair
enough...these are quite strong claims". Again, from the operational point
of view of the paper and from what's largely a subliminal attitude or
ideology that he is working from - he'd say, "its only one of these cranky,
environmental groups that is making the claim" so don't take it too
seriously. [LNJ]

The journalist above can anticipate the reaction of his supervisor
(the news editor) because he understands and is aware of the policy of the
organisation. He refers to the "subliminal attitude or ideology" his
colleague works from, inferring that there is an invisible, tacit formula
against which the editor evaluates and constructs the news. It is evident
then that some reporters are aware of a set of organisational norms which
causes them to perform the routine tasks in certain ways.

A consummate professional standing is achieved through the
compounding of a basic grounding in news practices and a number of

years experience. However, it is paradoxical that two of the fundamental requirements of journalism: instinct and common sense exist in harmony, due to the fact that they are opposing qualities (i.e. instinct suggests spontaneity and common sense, rationality). Surely, journalistic instinct is a learned phenomenon but it has been socialised and reinforced to such an extent that it appears instinctive. This suggests that journalists have tacit knowledge and abilities while simultaneously possessing this rationality which underlies the routine procedures carried out during the news process. When asked about these diverse qualities, the journalists returned to the subject of news sense.

> You develop a news sense and you can only develop it by working in it [journalism]. It may be that you are naturally inquisitive and you like finding out things. But you can be inquisitive and like finding out things and not be able to put it over in a way that other people can...communicate it. So it is a balance of having that inquisitiveness to find out things and having the ability to put it over so that people understand what it is. News sense is more than common sense rather than anything else. [LRJ]

> News sense is something which is developed with practice but I think you have to start with it. If you don't start with a basic news sense - a basic curiosity about something and then this urge to communicate what you have found out, if there is nothing of the gossip in you then I think you would have an awful difficult time. You could become a critic but even that...you've got to find a line, there's no point in doing it otherwise - find a line to make people read on. [EC(b)]

> Television and radio are exactly the same as newspapers. You are listening to what somebody says and you are picking up the news points e.g. a speech from John Major. If he's speaking for 45 minutes at the end of the day, it might end up as three or four paragraphs in the newspaper. It's constructed around three or four paragraphs so any journalist learns to look for the news line. You learn to extract the meat out of the story. It's something that's instinctive. It doesn't happen overnight. They don't start off with inexperience and say, "well that's how you do it". It's something you just pick up subconsciously. It is instinct. [LTJ]

Editorial and organisational policy

To a great extent, the selection of news is dictated by the management of the news organisation (Gaunt, 1990). This is due to a change in the ethos of news and news making. Gaunt argues that the organisations are working towards a more profit-oriented remit nowadays and that the selection of news stories is defined as those stories which are the easiest to edit. Early on in their careers journalists are instructed as to the values of the newspaper or broadcast organisation and indirectly, therefore, as to what values their stories should be reflecting. This strongly influences the way news is constructed. If stories are written which violate the policy, they will often not appear. The editor creates the editorial policy by taking into consideration the different requirements of each department in the organisation (paper or broadcast station). One journalist admitted that the newspaper he works for would ignore the hypothetical story about the air pollution and respiratory diseases (case 2). He rationalises the reasoning behind this decision by saying,

> It's not that the newspaper...is callous towards the environment and so it doesn't care about car exhausts or anything. In a situation like this...I mean everyone drives a car and particularly our readers drive big cars with big engines...so that's probably another reason why it's not on the agenda. But I mean that sounds as if the management structure rationalises that in a sense - "we-can't-call-for-cars-to-be-outlawed-because-that-will-alienate-our-readers". It's just built in - a subconscious thing - built into the culture of the organisation. [LNJ]

Implicit in this are, of course, the economic factors which academics like Gaunt (1990) say are now the driving force behind journalism today. The readership or audience and their interests are predominant considerations within the design of organisational and, therefore, editorial policies.

One journalist explained how the force of the news values, perpetuated by the organisation, determines how quickly the journalist adapts to the new work environment i.e. socialisation of the newsroom (Tuchman, 1972).

> I think if a BBC journalist, for example, went to work in a tabloid paper and wanted to keep his/her job there, that journalist would quickly learn that it pays to acclaim and that you really have to have opinions and in some circumstances you've got to express them. It's a different style of

54

journalism so ...it's learned. You learn the standards set by the organisation. Every organisation has standards - some codify the standards...some codify standards in forms...certain ways. [LTJ]

These standards are implicit in the organisational policy which manifest themselves in editorial policy. The editorial policy which journalists work to.

You have a line....but before that there's a style, that just happens to be...if you work on a newspaper the style is actually ingrained and you just do it. [LNA1]

This style is represented in the editorial policy and reporters are taught to conform to these standards in the newsroom. If the policy is violated, the stories are changed through editing or else do not appear.

Gaunt's idea that the media, specifically the newspaper industry is driven by profit seeking ideology, was echoed again by one of the journalists,

...if, for example, in this story, if a Peterhead fishing company was one of the worst offenders that was overfishing in the North Sea and they happened to take out a lot of advertising with us, that would be a consideration you know. If they threaten to take out their advertising if we run a really hard hitting story against them then I strongly suspect that the story would be pulled completely or it would be watered down.... [LNJ]

Newspapers and broadcast organisations help shape the news by reinforcing professional and organisational norms which are mainly economic in origin.

Professional and personal roles

Gaunt (1990) also argues that the journalist's professional role is determined by historical context, public expectations and organisational control and further that his/her personal role may be dependent on training, type of organisation, journalistic traditions, editorial pressures.

The journalists have very clear perceptions of their self-image, for in describing this image they specifically stated the roles which they see themselves fulfilling. From the evidence, there have emerged two professional roles (social responsibility and economic) and one personal role (self-criticism). This image is influential in shaping the rules which journalists use to construct and interpret the news.

Many of the journalists discussed the ways in which they would avoid sensationally publicising issues which would alarm the public. This is the journalistic role of social responsibility which is defined professionally and, therefore, has originated from both the organisational culture and the academic training programmes.

> The way you feel about something can affect the way it is constructed but I think it's the responsibility of the reporter to avoid making that happen. But newspapers don't have a legal responsibility in the same way TV has to be politically balanced. As long as it is not breaking any public order laws like inciting people to riot or racial hatred, a newspaper can print what it likes and they do. I think that it would be a falsehood to say that there is the ideal of the completely impartial journalist. [LNJ]

Historically, it has been suggested that the media violates its responsibility to the public and that it indiscriminately reports things in a dramatic and sensationalist fashion.

The social responsibility role of the journalist involves avoiding the conscious misleading of the audience or readership. For example, a negation of this responsibility may occur where a potential link has been stated as fact, such as assuming that the pesticide Benazalox has caused the illness of seven people even when these people are geographically dispersed around the area (case 1). Journalists cannot afford to draw conclusions based on their own speculation and commentary should be distinct and separate from factual reporting.

> A lot of the time you are trying to report what other people are saying, after all. You may have to contrast what they are saying to others but contrasting is a different matter, it's not the same as injecting your own stuff. [LNA1]

Most of the journalists talked indirectly about the role of social responsibility. Usually this was in the context of how they would avoid sensationally publicising issues or parts of issues which would cause alarm to the public. For example, placing undue emphasis on the fact that in case 1, the chemical pesticide may be carcinogenic. The journalists are very aware of the need to remain professional and responsible in matters where a scare might be caused. They see this need as an inherent part of their role and this consequently defines how they practice the routines involved in the news process.

The profession has apparently changed as journalists are now expected to assume more responsibility from an earlier stage in their careers.

> I am very mindful that everything should be very responsible...I think you must be responsible and not cause a scare when there's no necessity for it. On the other hand people will always tell you there is no cause for panic. You've always got to be responsible and quote the facts to get the balance. [NNJ]

The journalists saw themselves as having to fulfil an economic obligation within their professional roles. News making is run as a business, with reporters having to identify and construct as many newsworthy stories as possible in order to justify their place on the news team.

> I'm a senior production journalist - a producer who occasionally reports. I'm looking for stories; choosing stories to do, assigning stories to people. I oversee the production of these stories, ensuring their production quality, managing a team of people...and we're all trying to do a good job and beat the opposition. [LTJ]

Competition is strong in the news business between stations and between newspapers and the economic influences on the journalists are clearly defined.

Self criticism

This is a personal function which reporters perform in order to assess their own working practices. It is adopted in response to the need to constantly maintain a self-set journalistic standard.

> If you don't think about the reader then you will end up writing needless and nonsensical stuff . You've got to analyse your own stuff. You have to sit back and say what would interest me? [LNA1]

> As a journalist you can't afford to draw conclusions because you don't know. You've got to report and if there is some argument, you've got to report that. [LNA2]

Collectively, this function is defined within the perceptions of the self-image which journalists hold tacitly. The roles are difficult to separate because they are inextricably interlinked and consequently influence each other.

Self-image

The journalists found it difficult to discuss their perceptions of their image. It was evident that the journalists found it easier to describe their own image by stating their role and what this entailed, for example,

> I see myself, pretty much, as a straight forward reporter without any pretension such as editing a [local] newspaper or a national. We have to act responsibly and professionally otherwise our reputation crumbles and we lose...You are part journalist and part businessman and part diplomat. You have to be a kind of a salesman in many ways as well I suppose. I never really thought about it before. [LNA1]

This person discusses how he sees himself i.e. as unambitious from an editorial point of view. His self-image is linked to the professional roles of responsibility and profit-seeking. Instead of simply referring to himself as a reporter who can recognise and evaluate potentially newsworthy material, he sees himself as "a salesman", which emphasises the economic influences of his role. The need to sell papers on the strength of certain stories is a concept echoed by other respondents as the following substantiates,

> our role is to sell newspapers, first and foremost. It is a business. Then you can be pious and say you are informing the public and protecting the public's right to know. [LNJ]

The journalists see their roles and, therefore, their overall image as having different facets. They are aware that the product they construct has an effect on the news consumer (audience/readership), indeed the rules which are inherent in the news process are applied with an image of the readership in mind. The following journalist admitted, however, that he sees his role as shaping people's images and actively constructing their realities for them.

> [as a journalist]...what you are doing is shaping people's

reality...because...for example...if you were to ask people "what do you think of Neil Kinnock as a leader?" They'd probably say, "oh he's weak" or "oh he caved into the unions". And you say "well give me an example of his weakness" and they wouldn't be able to because their reality has been shaped by the newspapers, which for ten years told them that Neil Kinnock was weak. People's general understanding of most things is what they read in the newspapers and if that's slanted in some particular way then you are affecting a large section of public opinion. [LNJ]

This is part of the process which has been reinforced by newspapers and broadcast institutions over a number years. It is reality which has been constructed within a particular context.

An interesting thing about newspaper journalism is that people always want to speak to you when they think that you can tell them something, you know if there is a big murder or a big police thing - it's ok to be a journalist then but if there is a disaster the same people treat you with contempt as if you are the lowest form of life. [NNJ]

Journalists are aware of the image which is perpetuated by other media e.g. film, TV drama, literature and this influences how they perceive themselves to some extent. However, the stereotypical misrepresentation of the profession over a long period of time is generally incongruent with the self-image journalists possess. Their image is composed of the different roles outlined above - social responsibility, economic, self-criticism, social construction etc. This image becomes part of their social construction of reality i.e. world view. Consequently, this must have a bearing on how they perceive the world and how they mediate these fragments of reality to the wider social community. The news is not reality, only an image or interpretation of the same.

5 The Editorial Rules

Like other bureaucracies, news organisations are a combination of hierarchy and division of labour...This reflects their divergent demands - on the one hand, centralised co-ordination to assure smooth routines and consistent presentation, on the other, widespread interaction with a diverse and unpredictable environment to generate news. Overall authority and decision-making are concentrated in a relatively small group of editorial executives, below which is a large and diversified middle stratum of reporters and processors. (Tiffen, 1989, p16)

This short chapter is concerned with the procedures and rules which affect editorial decisions. As with all the other categories, the rule sets are used in combinations by journalists and consequently it is clear that these sets influence each other. For example, the constructional and interpretive categories are always used together as they are primarily concerned with the writing of the story (see chapter 8).

The editorial rules which appear in fewer numbers than any other category are distinct from the other rules because they play a different role in the news process. The news process can be described as a chronological statement but it is difficult to include the editorial rules in this statement. For example, journalists use the evaluative rules initially to assess the newsworthiness of an issue by weighing it up against criteria determined by the news values of the paper or broadcast organisation. The natural progression of this process is to implement operational rules for the purpose of gathering the information from sources including interviewing actors involved in the situation. In addition to this journalists apply constructional and interpretive rules to write or construct the story, for example, they include or reject bits of information, select particular quotes from experts or "victims", they "interpret", distil and, therefore, simplify information (including scientific and technical) for their readers. However, editorial rules are applied consistently at each stage of the news process. These particular rules also exist on a tacit level because journalists are aware to some extent of the routines which are involved in their work. Journalists learn about the editorial and, therefore, organisational policies of the institution through experience of the newspaper or broadcasting culture (findings which support Sigelman (1973). However, it is also learned by osmosis and what Breed (1955) calls the socialisation of the newsroom where new reporters are conditioned and influenced by work colleagues through a reward system. Novice journalists are trained, therefore, by a repetitive practice which reinforces the work in a positive way.

> ..they become socialized and "learn the ropes" like a neophyte in any subculture. Basically, the learning of a policy is a process by which the recruit discovers and internalizes the rights and obligations of his status and its norms and values. He learns to anticipate which is expected of him to win awards and avoid punishments ...he tends to fashion his own stories after others he sees in the paper. This is particularly true of the newcomer. The news columns and editorials are a guide to the local norms. (Breed, 1955, p328)

Editorial rules are outwith the control of the individual journalist. They are devised by the editorial team which is directed by the editor of the paper or news director of the broadcast organisation. Ultimately, however, the control of the policies, to which the reporters work, is kept by the publisher or the station manager. It is unclear as to what extent the publisher influences the direction of newsroom activities and, therefore, the ultimate shaping of the news. Work by Bowers (1967) shows that publisher activity is greater in smaller daily papers due to the fact that he/she is more involved in the community and with his/her staff and also because the economic resources of these papers are smaller. He also found that publishers who had risen from the editorial ranks were better able to use their specialist knowledge in the news policies and in the application to news problems (Bowers, 1967, p52).

The following schematic diagram illustrates the news process as a sequential statement.

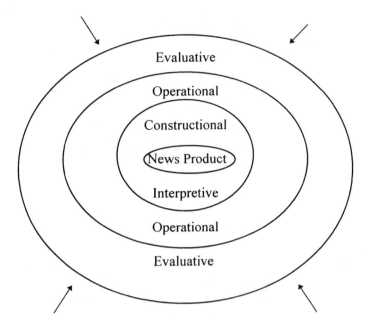

Editorial rules and influences ⟶

Figure 6 The Integration of Rule Categories

Although the diagram depicts the fact that editorial rules are the primary consideration which take place before the other categories, it should be understood that journalists are aware of editorial decisions while simultaneously carrying out the other tacit procedures within the news process. Through the socialisation process of the newsroom, journalists absorb the ways of working and this is influential in shaping the news product. They are not consciously aware of this because they found it difficult to explain. However, they are aware to some extent of how this influences them because they have all discussed how newsworthy or un-newsworthy the stories are in relation to their particular medium.

The editorial rules are concerned with the practical technicalities of the news process. This is due to the fact that the rules in this category are primarily concerned with how to fit the news into particular spaces within the newspaper or broadcast schedule.

> There would probably be more science in the radio piece especially if it is quite a long time. The television piece would be much more wedded to pictures of bodies of the dead animals, the countryside that we are referring to - very small soundbites of the scientists, or the farmer and the ill person. [EC(b)]

> It's difficult [to say] but I would be looking at a six minute piece and the initial one on this would be unlikely to run for more than six minutes. The follow up could take another six minutes...the general overview on the use of pesticides or whatever could be around a discussion which would last maybe ten minutes. [LRJ]

Some of the journalists were able to estimate approximately which case would appear on the front page but they qualified this by stating that this was subject to what other stories arrived on the day. This was an application of the evaluative rules in conjunction with their editorial knowledge. It is an example of one category influencing the other.

> It didn't fall off the bridge but it was de-railed? I'd say it would be on the front page for two or three days. I mean you can't tell because from this scenario, you can't tell if it's going to be sealed and carried off and you'll be left with a relatively small amount of fuel, and no scenes of dead ducks or seals washed ashore. So...from that it's difficult to say but certainly on day 1 it would be a front page story. [NNJ discussing case 5]

> It wouldn't be on page one. If you've got good pictures it might make page four or five. It would depend very much on the day - if we've got other stories running. They might just decide that they want a human interest story for that day and that would make it quite prominent but on the other hand there might be other stronger stories but it would be unlikely to make page one. It would be the inside pages. If it was a quiet day that might make page one because it has got lots of implications and many different strands. [EC1(n) discussing case 2]

The constraints placed upon the news process by editorial rules may be found specifically in the leader column of the newspaper. This is a method through which news organisations can support or oppose a particular lobby or other political situation. This is written by the editor and it is opinion led. One journalist's discussion of case 3 supports this,

> it is quite possible that it's the kind of story which the paper might write a leader on. It wouldn't take sides on the reporting of it at all...I don't think it's something they'd campaign on - But ...they could write a leader on it, expressing an opinion on it. I think it's a very difficult one to express an opinion on because the arguments sound simple but they're not terribly simple. And the ideal solution is not apparent. There's conflict between serving the community and the environment. I guess the leader initially... having looked at the amount of information on this since it was proposed...the view would be slightly skewed against the development. The leaders of course entirely depend on the opinion of the editor. If he disagrees with what I've written, he will re-write it. [EC2(N)]

Editorial revisions (Sigelman, 1973) is another example of one of the rules in the category. Sigelman found that journalists were able to anticipate the actions of their immediate superiors i.e. news editors (see also sources of rules, chapter 4). One journalist, discussing case 4, stated that he became aware that the fishing authorities should be given a more prominent standing in the story than would normally be given. This was due to the fact that the journalist had been advised by the editor to do this because of the newspaper's policy and so as not to alienate the readership (a large percentage of which work in the fishing industry).

> If it came in from this group then we would be quite interested in this. Particularly if it said that unemployment was going to result from it. I did the fishing page on my second week here, and I was doing stories as if they were hard news stories and I got so many complaints...we would probably use this but we would give the fishing organisations an equal if not greater say. [LNJ]

The journalists, then, apparently have little overall control over how the news story will appear in its final form. Furthermore, the news process is carried out under intense pressure caused by deadlines and the saturation of the work load by incoming material.

The editorial category is used in conjunction with other rules (operational, evaluative, constructional/interpretive) and that this is extremely influential within the news process due to the fact that all the other rules are implemented in the work routine with a knowledge of the editorial mechanism in mind.

What we are working towards is the timescale of the editions which doesn't necessarily fit in with or comply with the development of the story's natural course. So that's where newspapers become, in my view, dishonest...Because you are trying to get a story everyday, you are perhaps distorting the natural development of the story. You can go off at tangents depending basically on the requirements of the paper. [LNJ]

Journalists are inflicting an artificial code of practice onto real life situations. In other words due to the very nature of the news process the natural or real progression of the story is altered by the rigidity of the news routines and therefore a contrived representation of the situation is created. This is not to say that journalists set out with the intention of biasing or structuring the news in a subjective context. It is not a premeditated process. It is simply that the nature of the business is such that news can never be completely objective. This is because the process determines the fact that the news has to be set in a particular context, and that it has to be constructed and disseminated within a particular time frame.

The notion of a passive, comprehensive repository of official proceedings is economically unfeasible in its demands on space (especially with the proliferation of such proceedings), and in a more time-conscious age, readers are unlikely to consume the columns of print involved. (Tiffen, 1989, p18)

This extends not only to print but also to broadcast media,

TV news has many distinctive features. The first is the brevity of the verbal information presented. The text of a half-hour news service would not fill the front page of a broadsheet newspaper...The production of TV news is dominated by a "stop-watch culture"...Visual quality is at the heart of the TV news enterprise. The construction of stories centres on the gathering and editing of suitable newsfilm. (Tiffen, 1989, p22-23)

It is evident that the editorial category is distinct from the others due to the fact that these rules are used in conjunction with the rules in other categories. This category, firstly, illustrates the type of knowledge journalists acquire by osmosis and the socialisation of the newsroom. Secondly, it demonstrates the organisational constraints which shape and construct the news product and ultimately the readership/audience's perceptions of reality.

6 News Evaluation

The world in which we come to have knowledge about the world, is of a particular sort...order. Though the order is always evolving (or better, changing) and never absolutely secure, it does represent a particular constellation of social relations of a particular integration of the institutions of society.   The manner of integration, of organisation indicates and serves to reproduce particular priorities, values and interests. News that informs us of the world, from the perspective of any particular world, will reflect those priorities, values and interests. News, then, is not simply a "constructed reality" but instead a reality constructed within a particular social, political, economic ecology. (Rachline, 1988, p127)

This chapter examines the evaluative rules which journalists apply to environmental issues in order to assess their newsworthy potential. These types of rules are particularly relevant to the claims of the secondary stage of the model which places the news process of the preliminary stage within a specific reporting context (a disaster). The following cross section shows the relevant part of the secondary stage of the model.

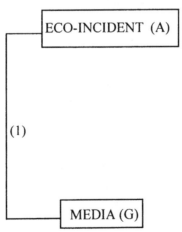

Figure 7 Excerpt from Secondary Stage of Model

This part of the model shows the media organisations dispatching reporters to the scene indicating that the story is newsworthy enough to warrant coverage. The evaluative rules are concerned with the news values and the news sense which journalists possess. This chapter addresses these issues and examines the categories to which news is assigned by journalists. The chapter begins with an experiment which involved the journalists prioritising and, therefore, evaluating the case scenarios presented to them.

Journalists approach to cases

Each journalist was asked to prioritise the five environmental case scenarios in an order which demonstrated the most newsworthy (1) through to the least newsworthy (5). This revealed the news values and related editorial policies of the paper or broadcasting institution.

All nine targeted media organisations took part in this prioritisation exercise, with the exception of a local news agency which supplies all main British newspapers with copy from the north east of Scotland and, therefore, could not be included. Four out of the nine journalists taking part in this section of the study were environment correspondents and the author wanted to perceive any differences between the ways in which specialists and non-specialists rated stories for newsworthiness.

It is evident that almost all of the journalists were able to rank the five stories in some kind of order. The exception to this, however, was the Scottish evening newspaper which would not consider the Cairngorm issue as this was outwith the area that would normally be covered and because no local angle could be perceived.

Table 1 How Journalists Prioritised the Case Scenarios

Cases	I	II	III	IV	V
Local News Agency	X	X	X	X	X
Local Newspaper	2	5	3	4	1
National Evening Newspaper[1]	3	2	X	4	1
National Newspaper1	3	1	4	5	2
National Newspaper2	5	4/5	3	1/2	1
National Sunday Newspaper	2	3	4	5	1
Local Radio	2	4	5	3	1
National Radio	2	3	4	5	1
Local Television	5	2	3	4	1
National Television	3	2	4	5	1

The data included in the table demonstrates that not all the respondents prioritised the cases in the same order. This is due to the fact that many of them work for different types of paper or broadcast institution and these have different news values. For example, the Scottish evening newspaper is a local paper, based in central Scotland, which deals with parochial issues and has a different set of criteria, against which to assess stories' news potential, from any of the other institutions.

The journalists, both specialists and non-specialists, recognised the importance of case 5 (environmental "disaster" type story) and rated it as the most newsworthy or as the story demanding the most immediate attention.

As the environment correspondent I would tend to choose the aviation fuel because you have got the public safety plus the pollution to the environment. There wouldn't be any choice if you had a disaster...you are bound to take the aviation fuel spilling all over the Firth. In a round up of the key stories, that would be a key story if it developed into a full-scale disaster - so that would be at the top of the running order. [EC(b)]

There's no doubt at all that the pollution of the aviation fuel is the biggest one. It's a national one. It's wider than just local. It's a big incident. There's lots of drama, lots of good pictures, lots of cuddly little seals who are at risk. That's definitely the main one. It's the only one of all these that I can think of that we would splash on. [ENJ]

Environment correspondents approach a story of this magnitude from a journalistic point of view first and an environmental point of view second. It is treated as a hard news story i.e. the facts of the case (what is happening at the scene) are followed up initially and later on attention is turned to the analysis of the situation (what are the environmental impacts). This is the rule for covering this type of story regardless of whether the journalist is a specialist or not.

> Tackling any story you would start by...whether you are writing as an environment correspondent or not...finding out what happened. You need to get the basic facts. You need to start off at the scene. [EC1(n)]

Table 1 is unrealistic due to the fact that it is unlikely that five environmental stories of such magnitude would appear in one news day. However, it shows that definite trends have emerged to the fact that the majority of the respondents prioritised the stories in the following way: case 5 (1); case 1 (2); case 2 (3); case 3 (4) and case 4 (5). The three most important stories (in news terms) were those which have the "hard"[2] news angles. Cases 3 and 4, although also environmental issues have less apparent news angles.

The selection of news stories depends very much on what other issues arise on that day and also the "subjectivity" of the editor's judgement. In using this term an implication of bias and personal construction is not intended. Much work has been carried out in the area of newsgathering and both academics and practitioners (Tiffen, 1989; Harris, 1989; Willis, 1991) maintain that the process is subjective. It is this knowledge which has led academics to label the subjective evaluatory process of news selection as "gatekeeping" (Lewin, in White (1964), p162). White in his study into wire editors' selection policies, states,

> through studying his overt reasons for rejecting news stories from the press association we see how highly subjective, how based on the "gatekeeper's" own set of experiences, attitudes and expectations the communication of "news" really is. (Lewin in White, 1964, p170)

If it is an accepted fact that news gathering is a subjective procedure, then this is further compounded by the rapidity of the news process. Editors make decisions without consultation because their experience and knowledge of the news process makes them the most appropriate people to do this. It is difficult to put forward any alternative to this subjectivity as it is inherent in the structure of the organisational norms.

> You may go to another journalist now and he may give you an opposite view [of prioritisation] and ten good reasons as to why it is an opposite view. You have to act on instinct and very often you are probably wrong but you have to act on instinct and make decisions fairly quickly. [LTJ]

This view that journalists use homogeneous rules in the news process is contradicted by the fact that there is an individualistic influence to the evaluation of news. It seems on the surface that this research into how journalists and news practitioners prioritise the news stories contests the ideas of hidden political agenda setting (Heeter [et al], 1989; Salwen, 1988). Having analysed the news process the conclusions may be drawn which suggest that news people possess a "news sense" which is learned, and is developed on the job. It is described by news practitioners as being an intuitive reaction which is used when assessing the relevancy of news for the readership or audience of their particular area. However, it is argued that if journalists were born with an innate, news instinct, they would report the news in the same way consistently. It is evident from historical analysis of news reporting e.g. the Chernobyl nuclear incident (Rubin, 1987; Luke, 1987; Friedman, 1987), that the Soviet Union's news coverage was distinctly different to that of Britain or the United States. It is possible that the socialisation of the news room and the reinforcement of the values which determine news sense are factors which probably contribute to the myth that this tacit quality is instinctive and therefore innate. Nevertheless, it is a reaction which news practitioners use when selecting news which is relevant for the readership or audience of their particular area.

> A story must have news value to stand-up and journalists have a keen sense of telling what is old-hat, propaganda or apocryphal. [LNJ]

> Most news reporters (and this includes environment correspondents) are expected to keep coming up with a stream of stories to justify their place on the team. Their success or failure is judged by the "by-lines" they get in the paper or bulletin. To succeed they need to develop a sensitive palate for news. This involves researching their subject area assiduously - scanning agency copy for new points of departure in running stories, browsing through periodicals for interesting snippets, scanning sheets of statistics, telephoning contacts or going to visit people and places - constantly judging new information against all known recipes for news

stories to see if it is worth further investigation. [JEd]

The journalist quoted above refers implicitly to the recipe knowledge discussed by Berger and Luckmann (1967). They proposed that knowledge is a social phenomenon which can be described and critically examined and that social actors (journalists) develop formulas to enable them to carry out their work strategies more efficiently.

> Everyday life is dominated by the pragmatic motive: i.e. to the solving of practical problems. Given the importance of this motive, *recipe knowledge* (i.e. "knowledge limited to pragmatic competence in routine performances") occupies a prominent place in our stock of knowledge. (Hunter, 1986, p15) (My emphasis)

This study set out to investigate the strategies which journalists implement during the news process. The understanding gained from this knowledge of the routine practices of reporters has provided a valuable insight into the ways in which the news is constructed as a product of what is assumed to be ordered reality.

The environment as a political issue does get relegated to the bottom of the running order or buried deep within the pages of newspaper text, because the media play a part in setting the political agenda, and the environment is positioned far down that agenda. Environmental issues are regarded from within the media as "soft" news stories although some journalists agreed that due to the recent popularisation of the environment as a subject in education, the media have had to start changing their attitude towards it.

> ...This year it [environment] is climbing the running order. It has always been "...and finally" and the sort of pretty pictures with the pseudo-scientific reason for running them and it still is that...It has suffered because it has been popular science and to make it understandable we have had to put pretty pictures on it and tell it in very simple terms that has made it quite simplistic in itself when in actual fact deep down it hasn't been. [EC(b)]

> ...There hasn't been a great deal of environmental coverage in Scotland until recently and even then there hasn't been a lot. There's a public interest but there's no real public involvement with environmental issues and that's something that I'm conscious of. Newspapers, and I include the Scotsman in this, tend to still treat the environment as a kind of "last item" on the news. They tack it on as a colourful, interesting, countryside

story which it is and it's not. [EC1(n)]

Environment correspondents suggested that environmental issues, were regarded as less important and less newsworthy, than other issues, due to their "softness". They also made it clear that these issues would often be approached by journalists in similar ways to other environmental stories which had been covered around the same time. The credibility of these other environmental stories was determined by association,

> ...stories like the M77 protest, the burning environmental issue - very accessible, central Scotland, so it's a big audience, it has been right at the top of the news. It has been *the* environmental story and from that kind of story anything else that has happened or has been attached to it, is suddenly being perceived as important. It is almost impossible to analyse what goes on in a news editor's mind. You start the year with a story like the M77 protest, which is an environmental issue and it is grabbing people, then it seems to follow from that, that other things which have a green tinge to them suddenly seem to become more important. [EC(b)]

Not only does this journalist suggest that issues which have received a great deal of coverage before, determine how related issues are treated in the future, but also that it is impossible to rationalise the apparent "subjective" prioritisation which takes place at the news desk. This journalist implies that, again, there is a randomness involved in the selection of environmental stories. Another reporter referred to this phenomenon as the "band wagon effect" which occurs when two or more similar incidents surface within a short time of each other. The second issue will trigger off a more intensive coverage because it is seen to be reinforcing a trend or pattern. It will be seen as topical and consequently it is magnified by the media at the time.

All the journalists prioritised the stories according to the news values of their particular organisation and in general no two orders were the same. Further, they all rationalised why they would have placed them in that specific hierarchy.

Journalists categorise stories. These categories range from the simple to the complex, in terms of content and in terms of how journalists gather the information for the story (see chapter 7).

> ...There's probably a range of stories and they range from simple, straightforward - going out and speaking to someone or on the phone...which doesn't really involve much in the way of alternative

sources or a complex story where you have to try and find out more information from the library. [LNJ]

From this exercise, the idea developed that the five stories could themselves be categorised.

Case 1 which dealt with the use of chemical pesticides in agriculture may be termed as a "serious incident" type of issue because it affects more than one person but its severity is not comparable with an "environmental disaster" story which demands immediate attention and usually threatens either large numbers of people or the eco-structure (as case 5 does).

Case 2 which was concerned with the worsening of respiratory diseases due to atmospheric pollution may be classified as an "action attempting to affect policy" story. If the link between asthma and traffic pollution could be proven this story would be stronger in news terms. Respondents seemed to disagree with each other about the real issue at stake. Many believed the action of the parents was the predominant issue, others felt that it was the fact that the girl had died (this is discussed later).

Case 3 referred to the development of a funicular railway through the Cairngorm mountains which was a continuing environmental issue. Respondents referred to it as "claim/counter-claim" story i.e. one side of the argument is represented first and then journalists report the other side, thus balancing the report. It is regarded as a straightforward if somewhat monotonous type of story to cover, by non-specialist correspondents.

Case 4 covered the issue of overfishing in the North Sea. This may be regarded as a localised environmental story which is of little interest to non-specialist journalists out-with the north east.

Case 5 is the easiest scenario to categorise and follows the pattern of environmental "disaster" stories. Specialist and non-specialist reporters cover this alike.

Table 2 Categorisation of Scenarios in News Terms

Case 1	"Serious incident"
Case 2	"Action to affect policy
Case 3	"Claim/counter claim"
Case 4	"Local story"
Case 5	"Disaster story"

All the stories are environmental and political due to the fact that they all involve Government intervention. Journalists all refer to Government officials in their list of sources for comment (chapter 7). The more newsworthy stories from a straight journalistic point of view are (in a hierarchy of importance), 5, 1 and 2. Cases 3 and 4 are generally regarded as less "hard". However from a specialist's view point, cases 3 and 4 have greater importance attached to them because the issues will have a greater impact on the environment in the long term. News is immediate. Scenarios which, for example, discuss the possible implications of a railway development on a conservation area or the idea that common fish stocks are dying out due to overfishing, are not seen as newsworthy as both issues would take a long time to develop.

> ...In environmental terms both the Cairngorms and the North Sea stories are far more important than all the others - all the others are on the day - strong news pegs but in terms of the future of Scotland - the Cairngorms and the North Sea would take priority but they are ongoing stories. It is very hard to pinpoint key turning points in these particular stories. [EC(b)]

The implications from this mean that specialist correspondents do not evaluate environmental issues from a specialist point of view. They approach stories from a news angle first of all, as the comments above and below suggest.

> In the overfishing, if the scientist was charging [that] North Sea fish stocks were irrevocably depleted, then that would be on a par with the train story. The train story could be the strongest. It is very visual. That is the most exciting news story. The overfishing story is however the most important story in the long term. [EC1(n)]

Journalists' categorisation of news

Tuchman (1972) argues that newsmen find it difficult to define news categories because they use them tacitly. Her work showed that journalists classify stories into categories labelled - hard, soft, spot, continuing and developing. The evidence gathered from the sample of journalists supports the idea that practitioners classify stories but the category labels which she has drawn out do not explain adequately the relationships between the categories which are used in combinations by journalists. For example, developing stories are hard as are spot issues i.e.

the label given to sudden unexpected events like disasters.

"Hard" news stories as regarded by journalists are current, relevant, consequential events that are usually affecting people and "soft" news stories have less relevancy and are perhaps not as current. One journalist explains the difference between the two categories.

> The difference between hard and soft news is that soft news is referred to as "puffing" - it's just verbiage...it's not important. It is not descriptive of what's immediately happening. Hard news is news as it happens and a reportage of events that are developing or happening. [LNJ]

HARD	UNEXPECTED
Developing	Breaking
Diary	Off Diary
EXPECTED	SOFT

Figure 8 News Categories Used by Journalists (after Tuchman, 1972)

The diagram illustrates the types of news, hard or soft and expected or unexpected. Breaking stories e.g. the Braer oil spill, are often categorised as hard, unexpected events; however, stories often change categories as they develop. For example, the Braer started as a breaking story but changed to a developing story when it ceased to be an unexpected event i.e. as it became normalised. Diary stories e.g. press conferences can be hard or soft and appear in advance. Off diary stories are generally classed as soft, unique events, human interest, which are unexpected. Tuchman talks about "routinising the unexpected" i.e. that journalists categorise events in order to be able to respond to them more quickly. Some of the journalists who were interviewed supported this idea by indicating that there are formulas that enable them to carry out the news process more efficiently. However, it is evident that the classification of news is but one factor used by journalists to formulate the news process and that the rules discussed in the typology, collectively enable reporters to research, construct and shape the news to fit the medium, more effectively.

The case scenarios that were presented to journalists can be classified according to the categories within the diagram. The collection of cases includes at least two examples of hard news (1, 5 and possibly 2 depending on the interpretation of the reporter). Scenarios 3 and 4 are regarded as soft issues by non-specialist reporters. Environment correspondents agreed that from the total of the five stories, 3 and 4 are the most important in environmental terms. However, due to the fact that they approach issues from a hard journalistic view point first and an environmental view point second, they too had to place the issue further down the news agenda. In addition to this, cases 1, 3 and 4 can also be classed as developing news stories.

> It [news] all comes under the broad church of news stories but some obviously are harder news than others, for instance, an oil spillage like the Braer is very hard news but possibly a report coming out about oil pollution would come lower down the schedule of news as it hasn't got quite the same impact. A human interest story about...thinking back to the scenario you painted about the child with the asthma...that's a different kind of news...it's more of a human interest story but it's still a news story. [EC2(n)]

Contextualisation

The fifth case was concerned with the derailment of a freight train carrying aviation fuel across the Tay Bridge. Many of the journalists mentioned that they were reminded of the Braer (Jan 1993) when confronted with this story. This is a reasonable expectation as many of the journalists in the sample covered the Braer spill. However, what happened was that some respondents started to describe how the Braer would be covered instead of hypothetical case 5. During the sessions, it was observed that the journalists, in uncovering the rules, were contextualising the imagined scenario with images of the Braer oil spill.

> You might find that ten days hence you've got a high death toll amongst some of the animals or as you had with the Braer some of the economic things - tainted fish and so on that would begin to come out. [EC(b)]

Some of the journalists mentioned the necessity for pictures of the seals before the incident and also afterwards covered in black oil, despite the fact that aviation fuel is colourless and much lighter in viscosity.

> You're looking at something on the scale of the Braer...31000 tonnes of deadly...I mean the Braer to some extent was heavy oil but and there was a storm which washed most of it away but here you are looking at a potentially huge disaster. [LNA2]

This seems to indicate that journalists take the procedural experience i.e. how they have previously carried out operational rules of a particular situation and apply it to ones they regard as similar. It suggests that journalists do in fact assign stories to particular categories. Furthermore, in using the same information strategies or routines for similar issues it may be deduced that reporters have perhaps a mental "template" which is used with other stories in the future. It is evident from the journalists' data that reporters use the same routines for particular story types e.g. "disaster", "serious incident" etc. and each time this comes into effect, the rules are reinforced more definitely.

All journalists seem to approach the stories in the same way indicating that they all view them from a hard news/journalistic angle rather than a specific environmental way. The differences which do exist between specialists and non-specialists are due mainly to the greater depth of knowledge about the subject matter which environment correspondents have, rather than the journalistic approach to the stories and the procedures which they employ during the news process (as discussed below).

Environment correspondents are not able to promote an environmental issue over a hard political or health issue. This comes back to the fact that the environment is regarded in news terms as a soft issue unless it has, for example, "disastrous" overtones i.e. criteria which push the issue up the running order or put it on the front page, a view also put forward by Hanson (1991).

There are differences also, as might be expected, between the press and the broadcast media in how they approached the stories and wrote case 1 as a news story. This is due to the fact that the logistics and pragmatics of the press and broadcast media are different in terms of time, space and presentation (Tuchman, 1969; 1978).

> You are taught a framework - how to balance a story by putting forward counter points of view, for example, how to cover the environment or district council. There are set parameters and certain steps. Routines are automatic. Things are obvious. You don't sit down and think what is the next step. You do it and you get faster through experience. [ENJ]

Journalists are aware, to some extent, that they use routine practices and that these have been reinforced through repetition. What is less obvious is that they use rules, many of which are tacit, to produce i.e. research and construct the news. The distinction between a procedure and a rule is implicit in the fact that the latter is a construct, shaped and structured by a number of different factors such as organisational policy and journalistic perception of the professional role. The former is less defined i.e. unrepeated, part of a method taught in academic training courses. The procedure used by journalists is the basis for the rule that becomes embedded in journalistic practice after the routinisation process where a certain length of time on a paper has been served.

> We have routine practices. We don't do things at random. You shouldn't have to think about it. It starts with the five "ws"[3]...you don't have to think about that after a while. It is something which is learnt and it is something which is instinctive. I think you can't wholly learn it. You must have an instinct for news. [EC(b)]

A more detailed discussion of the sources of these rules can be found in chapter 4.

The evaluative category, which forms the basis of this chapter, contains rules like news values and newsworthiness and provides the framework for the reasoning behind the prioritisation exercise where the journalists placed stories in a hierarchy according to their newsworthiness. "Evaluative" refers to the ways in which journalists approach stories initially, summarise the issues' news potential and assess the extraneous factors which strengthen or weaken a news story e.g. government intervention which strengthens an issue. Reporters are constantly making value judgements against the information using news criteria which are perpetuated by the organisation. However, this is not always recognised by journalists as a subjective process due to the fact that they do not analyse their own working patterns. Each of the journalists categorised the stories differently (page 68) and the reason for this was found to be due to the diverse news values sustained by each of the organisations.

> Journalists need stories that are recent and relevant to potential action by audiences and that have a local angle, human interest and an element of novelty. Reporters are under pressure to be "first" with a story, even when no event is making the information newsworthy. (Burkhart, 1992, p79)

The different parameters set by each news organisation makes it difficult to compare how journalists gather news stories, for example, an evening paper might have eighteen deadlines a week whereas a Sunday paper may only have two and a daily regional paper may have up to sixty. The Sunday paper, therefore, has a greater length of time to locate news stories. This, inevitably, has a bearing on how journalists evaluate issues, therefore, journalists use a set pattern of rules to help them evaluate and organise potential stories. These rules become so ingrained in the journalistic process that reporters can identify stories without consciously deciding to apply the evaluative criteria. Further, journalists use rules to classify the types of story they receive or locate. This supports the work carried out by Tuchman in the 1970s as similar results were discovered when the Scottish journalists had difficulties in describing the news categories they use. This was due to the fact that again journalists do not rationalise what they are doing during the news process. The rules are applied to the environmental issue tacitly.

News value rules

> ...Values are built up over time and generations...so the values are perpetuated and the news fits into that kind of narrow definition. News is not an abstract notion...it's something that clearly...people go in, in the morning and decide what's going to be news and what is not. [LNJ]

Much has been written to date about news values by practitioners and academics. These values are a vitally important component within the evaluative category. Although there are many different news values which differ from organisation to organisation, the journalists (from within the context of the five cases presented to them) revealed that geographic location and human interest were the most important. It was also discovered that "negativity" is a quality which determines a better news story although it is not included as a definitive news value criterion. In Scotland the media is small but diverse and, therefore, a regional paper such as the Aberdeen Press and Journal has very different news values from, for example, a national news network like the BBC. However taking this into consideration there are standard rules which journalists apply to each story to test its newsworthiness. The author is aware that academics have identified more news criteria during the course of their research (McNair, 1994; Hartley, 1982; Hetherington, 1985, 1987). However, the criteria identified here are the outstanding categories which the journalists revealed, whilst implying others such as proximity, immediacy, ethnocentrism etc. The reporters did not expand on these as they were constrained by the context of the information case scenarios and some values were, therefore, not relevant at the time.

Geographic relevance

This refers to the location of the story. An incident which occurs in Aberdeen, for example, the illness resulting from the use of chemical pesticides (case 1) is of less importance to a national evening paper than it is to a regional paper in the north east of Scotland, and this fact is reflected by the amount of coverage each paper or broadcast station gives it. The exception to this rule (discussed below) is when a "disaster" story such as the derailment of the aviation fuel train (case 5) takes place. Depending on the scale of the event, all media (press and broadcast) converge on the scene to cover the incident. A "disaster" being the most newsworthy type of story is regarded differently by journalists. It is the most easily recognisable in terms of hard news and the application of news value criteria is seemingly suspended and deemed as unnecessary during these situations. This is due to the fact that the scenario is very often strong enough to stand up by itself in news terms and there is greater urgency to communicate the facts.

For example, a story such as the one described above ("disaster"), often does not need an Aberdeen line i.e. mentioning the name of the area to justify its place in the schedule (case 5).

> There is no great need for me to say anywhere, the fact that it was on its way to Aberdeen. If it was on its way to Aberdeen and it's carrying twenty dignitaries and they all got dumped in the river then it's on its way to Aberdeen. But [in this case] the fact is secondary. [LRJ]

The addition of the human component adds strength to the story, and the Aberdeen line is necessary to help the listener make sense of the issue. However, this story (case 5) is strong enough to stand without the mention of Aberdeen.

The journalists further described why geographic criteria strengthen a news story, from within the context of case 1,

> if it happens in the North-East then that would be important. If they were from the North-East then that would make it even more important. If the people were from outside the readership area it would make it less interesting to us, but the fact that it happened in the North-East would certainly make it relevant. [LNJ]

> In this case I would say that the "Who" is probably the most important thing and also the fact that there is a specific geographical location. You have to remember that news values tend to impinge a lot. It varies geographically. A provincial paper like the [Aberdeen] Press and Journal...this is a big story for them as this is the local patch, but in terms of the national press for which I work predominantly, it's not a big story unless it happens to be affecting people in other farming areas of Scotland. [LNA2]

Location, then, has a very definite bearing on whether or not the journalist would cover it. This is linked to their images of the intended audience. It is evident that journalists are very aware of the audience or readership they are writing for (see chapter 8) and the geographic criterion is applied automatically to ensure that the news story is of relevance to the news consumer. The discussion of case 4 underlines this,

> ...that is a major story for our area because the fishing in decline though it is, is still a major part of the life of not just the North East but of Orkney and Shetland and the Western Isles, all of which is part of our transmission area. As long as you've got the industrial side of it, you've got the fishing processors and you've also got something the housewife, be she in Aberdeen, Dundee or Inverness, can relate to. [LTJ]

> There are knock on effects right through out the area. This is the type of story that we would be very interested in. If we take away North Sea oil...what are the key industries of the North East economy...fishing, farming, papermaking etc. A lot of them have gone into decline. Fishing and farming are still rock solid in our transmission area. [LTJ]

In contrast, the issue is not important at all to the non-environment reporter from the central belt,

> I don't think we would cover this....we would probably have to see if there was any local angle on it. I think most of our fishermen, fish further south than the North Sea. If there are people who fish in these areas then you have a local angle. But because it's not as important around here as an employment area, it wouldn't be quite as important as it would to the Express or the Press and Journal, for example. [ENJ]

Human interest

The journalists, who were interviewed, unanimously agreed that in being confronted with a story initially, they assess its newsworthiness by identifying who is involved in the scenario. In case 1, it is indicated that in total seven people around the Aberdeen area are ill and it is implied that the cause is chemical poisoning. All the journalists in the sample agreed that the top line of the story i.e. the predominant news angle, would be the fact that humans had been affected by a pesticide and that they were ill. The broadcast journalists made these comments,

> ...that is a fairly hard news story. It's affecting people and it's affecting animals and it is an issue which people would be interested in...because there is a suggestion that it has been caused by chemicals which have got into the water supply. [LRJ]

> This story as with any story would be dictated by news values and these values do vary from journalist to journalist and from institution to institution. In broad terms there is a kind of priority scale against which facts are assembled. The fate of a person is usually inherently more interesting than the fate of an animal although both may be important and both would certainly be reported here. However I would certainly report that people were ill before I reported that animals had died unless I found that hundreds of rabbits and foxes...had died and only a couple of humans were affected and that there were doubts to what the link was. [LTJ]

There were no differences perceived between the press and broadcast journalists nor between specialists (environment) and non-specialist reporters, with regards to the way they approach stories. The assessment of news story potential is a standard rule, universal to all types of reporter, as the following shows, if I had to write a story based on this particular press release, it would be the fact that humans had been struck down by what appears to be some sort of poison. The fact that animals had been found dead...would be pretty high up but it wouldn't be the main point of the story...when you're doing a story like this, then your main concern is that if there are animals or humans, humans come first. [LNA1]

...The most important thing is the human aspect of it, the fact that there are people who are ill. First and foremost we would go for the human element - the fact that people are ill. There's a suggestion, even though it's not confirmed, that it could be caused by pesticides or toxic chemicals they work with, so from a news point of view that would be our major interest. [LNJ]

In contrast to the first case, which was classed as a "serious incident" type story, case 3 was constructed in a completely different way. An examination of the journalists' responses to case 3, demonstrates how differently reporters evaluated the issue.

The third case was referred to by the journalists as a "claim-counter claim" story which indicated the way they would cover it i.e. balancing a claim with a counter claim from the opposition. The scenario described the proposed development of a funicular railway, which would run to the top of one of the Cairngorm mountains, transporting a large number of additional visitors. Mixed responses were received from the group of respondents. Firstly, not every reporter would cover it, for example, a journalist from one of the national newspapers refused to use it due to the fact that it was outwith his readership area. Therefore, the geographic relevance rule underlined the fact that the story was of no interest or relevance to his readers. Secondly, some reporters indicated that due to the absence of any human angle the story was weaker than either of the two previous cases.

There's no human angle on it. That's one of the main problems. Unlike the last scenarios, where there was a human face, nice pictures, nice quotes and things. There's no human angle on this unless you've got some granny who is going to be shoved out of her house because of the plan. There's no human angle. [ENJ]

It is an interesting story...but there is no specific human angle there. It is a company announcing a plan, so you report the announcement of the plan because it does have implications on, for example, tourism and the environment but it doesn't have as the various other ones have had, the death element or whatever. It is a good story and it is worth running. [LRJ]

These journalists believe that the issue is good i.e. worthy, because it is local and yet it is weaker than the first two cases because it lacks a human interest angle. It may be suggested then that although one of the most important factors which can be used to evaluate a news story is the human element, its newsworthiness is still dependent on the type of story being assessed and its location. The news values appear to complement each other. All the journalists had their own ways of prioritising stories and the main rationale they gave to justify their decisions was that the audience or readership are familiar with a particular type of order.

> I prioritise the stories so that people know what to expect. They know that the first story in the bulletin is going to be something that is going to hit them. Equally they know that towards the end of it they might get...a cosy story to finish off with so that they feel quite good about it. And then the music starts again.... [LRJ]

This journalist describes a typical radio news bulletin, but his comment can be applied to the television and print media, as readily. He underlines what the other journalists implied, that the news is arranged for the audience and readership. This point crystallises the fact that the journalist is influenced by not only the policies of the organisation and his/her training or experience but also by images of the intended audience. In journalistic terms, the reporters believe that case 3 was of average importance i.e. it was prioritised from position 3 downwards (page 68) because there was no human angle (as there was with case 1) nor any dramatic quality (as there was with case 2). However, it was clear from the data that the environment correspondents rated it as being one of the top two most important issues in environmental terms, even although they were unable to promote it over and above the "harder" news stories i.e. cases 1, 2 and 5.

> ...The main thing...the top line would be if they were sufficiently ill. I think I find the frustration for me, in being an environment correspondent...if it is a toss up between a health story in one programme and an environment story, the health story nearly always involves people and illness and death and that seems more newsworthy than birds dying or things about the long term future of the Cairngorms. If children are being

turned away from a Paediatric ward today at a hospital then, that is obviously going to take precedence over Scotland's wildlands in 20 years time. My top line would be that people are reported as being ill. [EC(b)]

Other journalists in the sample agreed that the issue was a worthy story, although the television journalists seemed more willing to consider it, due to its visual qualities.

It is the classic confrontation between environmentalists and ourselves...the Cairngorms is an area right in the middle of our transmission area. It is something which along with the skiing industry brings great wealth to the area and employment as well, so it is obviously of interest to us. [LTJ]

It is an extremely visual story with all the mountains and scenery and the wildlife as well...you've got mountain hares around Ptarmigan and a whole manner of interesting things. You've got a very, very good story because you've got people who feel passionately about the subject. [LBJ]

In discussing the visual qualities of the story, the above journalists have also indicated that the issue can be covered with a human interest angle. The employment which may be created if the development takes place and the environmentalists who put forward a strong case in opposition to it are both angles which these journalists maintained would become apparent in their coverage.

You've got the environmental considerations and we have readers in this area who have a stake in maintaining these because they have big houses and they like the view. On the other hand, you've got the promise of jobs - so in a situation like this you've got an unholy alliance of campaigners and middle-class homeowners which is a pretty powerful lobby. As far as the story goes it would be a good one for us. [LNJ]

Regardless of what type of news organisation journalists are affiliated to and regardless of what issue is to be covered, in journalistic terms practitioners always follow the human interest angle first. This is a standard rule which is used repeatedly.

Negativity as a news quality

News values are of differing kinds. Unlike the other two criteria (geographic and human interest) negativity is not a rule which journalists apply to an issue to test or assess its newsworthiness. Rather it is a quality which is generally although not always, inherent in a hard news story. It is not a recognised, necessary prerequisite for a news issue but it is a phenomenon that is almost synonymous with newsworthiness. Three out of the five news stories presented to journalists can be classed as negative (1, 2 and 5), the other two can be categorised as neutral. It is interesting to note (see table 1, page 68) that cases 3 and 4 (Cairngorms and overfishing) are the scenarios which appear most often towards the lower end of the journalists' hierarchy i.e. the least newsworthy. This is despite the fact that the environment correspondents rate them as being the more important issues.

Some of the journalists referred to the campaign Martyn Lewis launched about good news that attempted to challenge the ways in which the media tend to concentrate on negative news. But many of the journalists, interviewed, indicated that the reason for the news being so negative was to satisfy the audience or readership's desire for tragedy and disaster.

> Newspapers tend to pick the negative aspects of an issue. I don't think it is a deliberate thing. Nobody's interested in things going along normally and there are far more things go wrong than go outstandingly well. [NNJ]

> Probably in over 50% of the cases...it is bad news rather than good news. A good story is someone who has been killed in a car crash or someone who has died in a helicopter tragedy. I would say that 70% of our stories are written about the negative things. People want to read about other people's misfortune. [LNA2]

The absence of an audience study makes it impossible to come to any conclusions about whether this is true or not. The journalists may be justified in attributing negativity to the consumers' desire for social trauma, however, this also may be just a myth perpetuated by the media to ensure the commercial success of news. This also forces us to beg the question, if over 50% of issues are regarded by journalists as being negative and therefore newsworthy, do reporters regard "neutral" or positive stories less seriously? Is this why environmental stories, which do not frequently possess dramatic or tragic elements, are often relegated to the lower parts of the schedule or paper? The degree of negativity within an issue can apparently also affect how journalists write the story.

> From an operational point of view... I can't get worked up about a good news story. Instinctively, it doesn't interest me so...unless it is something like a big jobs boost but even in that I don't enjoy writing about it in the same way I do, writing about disasters and tragedy. If you are asking me whether as a newspaper person would I concentrate on the negative aspects then I think the answer is, undoubtedly, yes. Good news stories are termed under the generic term "puffiness". Anything which is verbose or is not hard news is just "puff". [LNJ]

In effect, then, negativity is a factor that can strengthen or "harden" a news story. Good news stories or neutral issues are regarded as "puff" or "soft" and are rated as having less value or credence, in news terms. Case 2 described the scenario where an eight year old girl died of an asthma attack and her parents blamed the increased amount of air pollution caused by traffic fumes. The journalists commented on the fact that the story was hardened by the girl dying. There was disagreement, however, as to whether the predominant news angle is the fact that the girl has died or the fact that her parents are starting a campaign about the problems of air pollution and respiratory diseases. Some believed that it was one and not the other, some decided that both factors were of equal importance and made the story newsworthy, others believed that there was no story because of the tenuousness of the link between the death and the levels of pollution. There were no significant differences between the broadcast and the press reporters, however, non-specialists were more likely to disregard this issue as unimportant than were the specialist journalists who recognised the relevance of the story as being one of the top environmental concerns.

> The fact that the child has died does make it more newsworthy and the fact that her parents are going to start a campaign makes it hugely newsworthy...The problem with a lot of environment stories is that you are always talking about such long time lags. It's "if nothing is done, then, in ten years time we could have the following results". Who cares what's going to happen in ten years time? [EC(b)]

This reporter underlines the fact that, again, one of the qualities or values which changes information into news is "immediacy". However, this is one news value which the journalists implied rather than stated.

87

News dates quickly, and this may be a reason as to why the environment is regarded as a soft issue - because it takes time to develop. This point was illustrated by non-specialists reporters who indicated that the issue is made relevant to the audience or readership through the fact that the girl has died.

> Because it is topical and relevant, this would be a good story...especially because you have got this dry, rather drab link between air pollution and asthma which is a good story but it doesn't grab people's interest. Then you've got an eight year old girl who's died...[which] is the hook on which you can hang all that scientific debate, that you've probably given one or two paragraphs in the past or maybe a health feature. You've suddenly got a news hook for it. [ENJ]

The issue is dressed up with drama and tragedy (see chapter 8) but the story is strengthened because the child has died. This point is echoed by another journalist,

> if they had said, "our daughter isn't very well because of increased traffic problems", yes we might consider it, but if they say, "our daughter died because of increased traffic"...it gives it a strength that it might not otherwise have had. [LTJ]

Several of the journalists stated that the story is too weak to be used as it stands. One journalist explained what factors would strengthen it,

> It is not a news report because it is not a news story. It has an element of a feature about claims that pollution is exacerbated asthma problems and endangered life...Basically, I could make a good story out of that but and it sounds very callous to say but I would prefer to get somebody else who had died where the doctor involved has said that there was a direct link. This is "usable" but it is potentially shaky. The issue's a good one, and there's a lot of concern about it. [LTJ]

Negativity may not be intentionally emphasised by journalists, but it is nevertheless one of the main factors which highlights stories' potential newsworthiness.

Relationship of news values to writing

When reporters are writing their stories they are still applying editorial and evaluative rules. The evaluative and constructional categories influence each other because journalists construct the news according to their perceptions of the news values perpetuated by the organisation. The journalists expressed the idea that the way in which they write is curtailed or constrained by the news values of the paper or institution.

> The way I write is in a sense curtailed by the news values of the paper. A tabloid paper would probably give more space to human interest stories whereas we might give more space to a story that has either economic...well for instance the Cairngorm Chairlift story scenario that you put forward...that would probably make three paragraphs in *The Sun* or *The Record* if it was used at all and a paper like *The Scotsman* or *The Herald* would probably give far more space to it, looking at the jobs versus the conservation issues, looking at the background to it, speaking to the people involved...that would be seen as a reasonably important issue for Scotland, where you put the interests of tourism raising revenue and job creation before the possible long term impacts of conservation but a tabloid is unlikely to devote much space to that. [EC2(n)]

> The way I write is probably curtailed by the news values of the paper. After a while you don't notice it. But the values are more or less the values of the people in the North East of Scotland...whether you believe they read [the paper] because it reflects their values or whether you believe that [the paper] shapes their values [is another matter]. [LNJ]

The journalist, above, admits that after having worked at the institution for a reasonable amount of time, journalists are no longer aware of writing in a particular style and this comment underlines the fact that many of these rules are tacit.

Through the repetitious constructional procedures (see chapter 8), inherent in the news process, the news values of the organisation are constantly reinforced and become the socially accepted norms of the readership or broadcast audience. Some of the journalists believe that the values of the readership and therefore their perceptions of reality are shaped by the newspaper/broadcasting organisation. For example,

> people's general understanding of most things is what they read in the newspapers and if that's slanted in some particular way then you are affecting a large section of public opinion. [LNJ]

Values are perpetuated through the journalistic rules or procedures and the news has to fit into the narrow definitions set by editorial and publishing policies. Due to the fact that these values are implicit in news construction it can be suggested (for there is no concrete evidence without an effects study) that readers/viewers/listeners receive a partial and fragmented view of environmental reality. Some of the journalists stated that news is not abstract but is constructed within a narrowly defined context by people who make conscious decisions as to what will make news and what will not. Furthermore, it was suggested that these practitioners subjectively prioritise and categorise news for the readership. The fact that a story is small does not necessarily mean that there is a lack of information about the subject. Someone has made a conscious decision to limit it to a particular length in order to fit in something else which in their opinion is more important in terms of newsworthiness. Case 5 is rated as the most important by the journalists but ironically the human element, which they maintain is the most important news value, is indirect in this scenario. This is due to the lack of individuals (victims) involved. The story stands as the strongest because of the potential environmental damage which might ensue and the dramatic re-telling of the event.

News values, therefore, affect the way stories are written but it is also evident that the personal views of the editors have some bearing on the construction of news as well. Some of the journalists pointed out that the editors at certain papers will include stories on topics which interest them specifically.

> It's a good story. It's a very straightforward one. It would probably take a trick with some of our customers but it's not one which would require a great deal of thought nor a great deal of time. It's easily written and the issues are pretty black and white. [LNA1]

How do journalists and editorial staff know what makes a newsworthy story? They possess what they call news sense.

Journalists' news sense

News practitioners all appear to possess a quality that they use to, not only, select news stories, but also, to determine the strengths and weaknesses of issues. This news sense may be partly inherent in an individual journalist's nature, but it is more likely to be a learned phenomenon due to the fact that the journalist develops it over a period of time on the job. This evaluative ability which is shaped and influenced by the organisational and editorial policies (see chapter 5) becomes implicit in the working practices of the journalist. News sense is, therefore, the ability to evaluate an issue and estimate its newsworthy potential. This quality is tacit or part of the news process that reporters do not think about but carry out automatically. It becomes like this because of the repetition of the same standard strategies or rules that are inherent in the journalistic process. The news value rules, discussed earlier are, therefore, implicit in the routinised practices common to journalism and when they become tacit after a period of time, they are regarded as news sense. This underlines the fact that journalistic news sense is a socialised and, therefore, learned phenomenon. The journalists found it very difficult to rationalise about news sense and some could not describe the phenomenon, indicating something of the tacit nature of these values,

> it is something which is learnt and something which is instinctive. I think you can't wholly learn it, you must have an instinct for news. For example in case 5 - the train, if you didn't have an innate news sense you might think that the fact that seals were being affected was the top line and over look the fact that humans might be affected. [EC(b)]

News sense is subjective in that journalists evaluate potential stories from within the context of the organisational norms. The journalists evaluated issues in completely different ways and they also assessed the factors that would strengthen a story in different ways. Case 4 was not regarded as being a hard news story by the journalists, due to fact that it was not a new issue. However, the specialist correspondents and local i.e. north east (Scotland) non-specialist reporters were more likely to treat it seriously as a potential news item. All journalists would cover the story providing it was strengthened by the release of a scientific report. The reporters pointed out that careful checking is done (see chapter 4) to investigate the origins of the press release claims. Furthermore, it is obvious that journalists approach and regard scientific researchers differently to environmental groups. They have an apparent implicit faith and respect for the former which is not replicated for the latter, a view also stated by Friedman (1986).

> This is kind of a difficult one to cover from a news point of view because you have to assume that there's some sort of news angle to this. It's not actually explained. If it is the case that some definitive study has said that stocks of haddock or cod are declining to the point at which the

environment is damaged...then it's an interesting story. If, on the other hand, it's Greenpeace or WWF saying that stocks have declined to a point at which the environment is damaged, then, it is a slightly different story. [EC2(n)]

This is a good issue because fishing is a main issue around here, so I would assume that this would develop from a marine scientists report. There are a few stories - environment, political, unemployment etc. but these are all might-bes, could-bes, so they're not as hard as if we had heard that a factory in Peterhead was closing and having phoned the guy up, he says its down to overfishing. That would make the story stand up better. [LRJ]

The journalists evaluated each scenario in the same way. Similar patterns emerged as they revealed which factors would make the issues more newsworthy, for example,

...if this happened in the North East where two people were on the verge of death because they had eaten food or they were working with crops which were sprayed with pesticides, then on the face of it, it's a good story and depending on developments it could be a great story - like for example if the pesticides were banned in this country or other countries that would be even better...that's the sort of thing that we would be looking at. The different lines we wouldn't get in one day. The first thing we would do would be to go for the human angle, to get photographs of the people. [LNJ]

In describing the possible development of the scenario, this respondent mentions all the main news values discussed above - geographic relevance, human interest and negativity in which illegality is included - all qualities inherent in newsworthiness. Negativity is implicit in the comment and the journalist uses the phrase, "on the verge of death" which is not stated within the scenario. It is unclear as to whether the journalist above is simply hypothesising about how the issue would be strengthened if the case was serious enough to have a reference to death or if he would interpret the story at this level. The others have indicated that issues are prone to being over emphasised i.e. amplified by journalists because they are directed by editorial staff in this way. Journalists are trained to expect the worst possible scenario and to overplay "disaster" situations rather than underplay them. This happens despite the fact that journalists have a keen sense of social responsibility (see sources, chapter 4). Evidence suggests that it is easier to admit in retrospect that a situation turned out to be not as dangerous as estimated at the time, than to have covered an issue moderately and to find out that the incident was worse than anticipated. This happened during the Braer oil spill where the media coverage escalated with saturation campaigns which led the readership or audience to believe that the situation was worse than it was.

> ...It has just happened so we wouldn't at this stage know how far it was going to go. It could turn out to be like the Braer...not too much of a disaster after all but you wouldn't go on that basis...you would assume that it was going to be bad. [ENJ]

The assumption of news editors that an oil spill is of the proportion of the Exxon Valdez or Braer has been reinforced by this rule of overemphasis. Journalists think about issues in terms of what similar stories they have covered before and this reinforces how they approach them.

Another factor was the apparent indiscriminate use of the term "disaster" (a key finding in the Braer case study) (Campbell, 1996). Journalists used the term casually when referring to the case (5). Historically, academics have accused the media of making value judgements through the language used to write articles (Bell, 1993; Fowler, 1991). However it is possible that journalists refer to situations as "disasters" because this is a label which has been assigned not only to a particular type of story but also to a particular way of reporting and consequently this has become normalised through its repetition over time. This together with the overemphasis rule of reporting "disasters" has been reinforced and routinised by the socialisation of the newsroom. Breed's (1955) hypothesis suggested that newsmen learned the policies of the organisation by osmosis and that these policies were reinforced by rewards from colleagues. This has been examined by Donahue (1967), Tuchman (1969) and has been previously examined in the sources of the rules (chapter 4).

Many of the journalists did assume that case 5 would be a "disaster", and seemed to have differing perceptions of the scope and magnitude of the incident,

> ...this is a major, major story. It's almost another Tay Bridge Disaster. It's a bit like the Braer in a sense. You've got contamination in the atmosphere, so again, you would concentrate first of all on the effect on humans and secondly on the effect on animals. [LNA1]

Very few of the journalists (only two) did not refer to the case as a "disaster".

> ...It goes back to what we were saying about the Braer. People were saying it was a disaster but we had not said that ourselves. It was a "massive oil spill". If we were explaining about the effects we would explain that seabirds were being washed up with the oil and that later seals appeared to be affected...but then again that is the difference between fact and judgement...we all have our views and we might think it is a disaster but we would not report it as being a disaster...so we all have a feeling for how we should approach the story. [LTJ]

It is clear that this type of policy is dependent on the organisation and is reinforced by editorial practices. Case 5 is different to the other four scenarios. It is a situation where all media would cover the event in spite of their differing news values. This is a definite example of news coverage overtaking ethics or training which is underlined by the following:

> ...the last one is definitely a good story. This is the kind of story which would get the pack out...which probably hasn't been true of any of the ones before. There would be individual interests in those ones [previous cases]. This one - all the press would be there. [ENJ]

> There would be no policy considerations at the paper about stepping on anyone's toes. Clearly in a situation like this...in "disaster" situations, the kind of normal operations of politics go out the window. [LNJ]

It is one of the "hardest", if not the "hardest" types of story, which consequently assigns it to top priority listing on the news agenda. The journalists indicated that relevancy, whether it is geographic, social or cultural is one of the most important news values. However, in cases like this normal news values are suspended.

> The more relevance it has to more people, the more important it becomes. This is a good story and it affects everyone. This is an environmental disaster which people are interested in because it happened in Dundee, but it might have happened in Aberdeen harbour - it did happen in Shetland. There is a relevance and where it happened is almost immaterial. [LRJ]

This is an example of the same kind of reasoning as occurred at the time of the Braer. The journalists contextualised this scenario (case 5)

94

with the Braer in the same way they contextualised the Braer with the Exxon Valdez (Campbell, 1996).

> You would just get a whiff of it [the story] and people would say "oh it's another Braer or another Valdez - let's get someone up there". [ENJ]

Normal editorial policy is apparently suspended in this situation and new criteria apply (see editorial rules, chapter 5). News values too are seemingly disregarded; however, it appears that operational rules e.g. contacts, interviews and constructional rules e.g. writing the story are constant no matter what the situation is.

The pragmatics of evaluation

The practical constraints of the news process affect the ways in which journalists evaluate news. Tuchman (1972) stated that the routines of reporters were affected by the constraints of time i.e. deadlines and space i.e. news holes in newspapers and schedules. This is more apparent in the broadcast industry where news appears to be more superficially covered than in the press, which has both the time and the space to include greater depth of analysis. News values are likely to be affected by pragmatics such as these,

> ...because it is a picture medium we are looking for a story that lends itself to pictures. If you are producing a half-hour magazine what you cannot do is start with a talking head, have a talking head all the way through and end with a talking head. We are actually looking for stories that lend themselves to visuals, but that doesn't mean...that we would ignore a story that would not lend itself to visuals. We try as much as possible to illustrate them and try to break it up and make them more interesting and to hold the viewer's attention. [LTJ]

The broadcast news team is picture-led and has to be aware of how a story will look or sound, than the press. With a radio broadcast the language has to compensate for the lack of visuals so a radio news bulletin's top line (headline) has to stand out more dramatically than a story in the press or on television.

> ...It gets people listening to things and that's always what you've got to do. Your first line of any story has to grab people. [LRJ]

95

Tertiary stage of model

The evaluative category has been concerned with the initial assessment of the environmental issue. The tertiary stage of the model (see page 97) describes how the journalist approaches the issue from within particular contexts. These contexts are defined as news values, for example, human interest, geographic relevance etc. Journalists evaluate environmental issues differently according to the policies of their organisation and where they are positioned geographically in relation to the issue/incident. It is with this knowledge that they can classify or categorise the stories in news terms e.g. whether something is hard or soft, developing, continuing or breaking. This leads to assessing the position of the story on the news agenda although it is dependent on the incoming stories on the day. The fact that an environmental issue may also lack dramatic emphasis has a bearing on how newsworthy an issue is, perceived by journalists. However, this is only one factor that usually relegates the environment as an issue to the lower end of the news schedule. These types of issue are regarded as soft, by the news media, partly, because the environment involves long term scientific research and often little change is appreciated over an extended period of time, and partly, because even although it is beginning to be realised as a political issue it is still viewed as a populist political issue. It may be argued that the media itself is to blame for the perpetuation of this populist perception because that is the way the environment is covered. The news sense which journalists use to evaluate environmental issues is deeply tacit as are the constructional/interpretive ones. It is the operational factors (see chapter 7) involved in the news process which are less tacit. They are tacit in that the journalists are less aware of the routines involved in the story investigation and of the methods used to verify links for example.

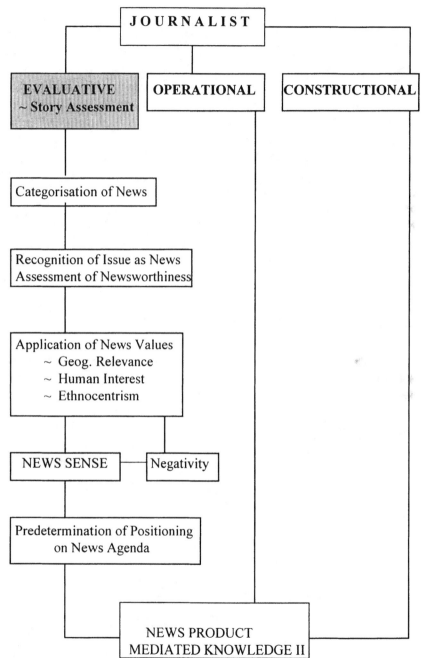

Figure 9 Tertiary Model: Evaluation

However, there is a greater awareness of the information gathering procedures and the contacts selection process. This is a subtle distinction not highlighted by the model. This chapter explains, through the tertiary model, how the evaluative (news values) and constructional (writing) categories are inter-related and how journalists apply more than one set of rules to an issue at a time. This is a point not clearly defined by the model in its two-dimensional state.

The fact that reporters categorise news stories into different types has been considered in an effort to demonstrate the prioritisation process inherent in the evaluation of such issues. The important theme of contextualisation has been examined for the purpose of illustrating how journalists evaluate potentially newsworthy issues within a previous, similar, established context e.g. the Braer, within the knowledge of the Exxon Valdez. The discussion about news value rules was extended to give consideration to news sense. This phenomenon, although described by the journalists as innate, is more likely to be a learned experience which through the socialisation and reinforcement processes has become mythologised as being instinctive.

Inevitably, journalists are directed by the bureaucratic and organisational pressures of the newsroom, to get as many strong stories as possible for each edition or news programme. The evaluation practices although structured by standard journalistic rules, are also influenced by the limited amount of time and space factors. The pragmatics of the newsroom differ considerably from the idealistic training environment within which reporters are taught to write comprehensive, balanced articles, (the sources of these rules has been discussed previously in chapter 4). The next chapter examines the operational rules (such as contacts, interviewing, the news lines which are developed) which are inherent in the news process.

Notes

1. The term "National", in this table, refers to Scottish. All the media were Scottish.
2. This is explained below.
3. The five "ws" are who, what, where, why and when.

7 Operational Rules

The categories described in the typology illustrate the extent to which journalism is decision-based. Reporters are constantly deciding what to cover, who to contact, what information to include and what to reject. When questioned about these day-to-day operational strategies, however, journalists find it difficult to rationalise how they carry out these routinised decisions because they perform them tacitly.

The operational category is, like the others, decision-based and journalists use strategies to select and locate appropriate contacts to interview and to retrieve relevant background information. Contacts help to provide the structure of the route or information chain along which journalists travel when gathering information. Reporters use each other's contacts and further, that once one or two appropriate people for comment are located, the search for additional contacts ceases. This underlines the fact that the flow of environmental information is redirected by the news process and that as new meanings are added to this information the product evolves as an interpreted and simplified version of the original.

The operational aspects of the news process also are influenced by the integral images of the readership which journalists hold tacitly. Journalistic strategies, an inherent part of the operation i.e. the selection of the news angles (perspectives which dominate the story) which are most important are shaped and constructed taking account of the most influential groupings within the readership, for example in case 1 this is the farmers. These groupings will influence the types of contacts who are approached and the decisions that are made regarding which contacts are used.

Information strategies

When initially confronted with the cases, the journalists immediately summarised the issues i.e. they described the problems. This was done, at the beginning, before they started to say what they would do and who they would contact. It seemed to be a clarification process so that the

99

information contained in the case and background information sheet was logically organised and evaluated in news terms by each journalist. For example,

> ...the main thing is that it is going ahead and there is environmental objection to it. There is a potential jobs boost but in the [long] term it might be a waste of time because environmentally the place is going to be degraded....You only get that sense when you get the full details of the thing. [LNA1]

> ...It's all about access and improving access to the mountains and there's a lot who have very strong opinions about this. You could speak to the Chairlift company to hear their side of it and it would be interesting to know to what extent they are doing it purely on commercial grounds.... [EC2(n)]

Journalists, once armed with this mental image of the situation, then use the operational rules which are an integral part of the process, i.e. they visit the scene of the incident, question the "victims", interview the officials, describe the issue for the paper or broadcast media. It may be suggested that this initial mental image is refined and modified as the journalist proceeds through the information gathering process.

Journalists described how they intended to research the story i.e. what factors will be involved, who will be interviewed or contacted and what angles will be followed up. As one of the journalists suggested, it is a process that involves taking decisions as the individual journalist proceeds. This underlines the fact that journalism is not only a decision-based profession but also that much of the operational process can be classed as having a snowball effect i.e. where one line of enquiry can reveal another.

Each journalist's approach to the news issue is different. There does not appear to be a standard set of inductive rules for their approach to and reasoning of an issue. In case 2, for example, some journalists would approach the parents of the deceased child first and others the car manufacturers to challenge them about air pollution. It depends on how a journalist interprets the issue and prioritises the various angles involved. This interpretation in turn directs the contact selection process through which reporters are searching for appropriate interviewees who will substantiate their news angles.

There are, however, some information gathering rules that seemed to be common to all the respondents. The majority of the sample followed routines that appeared to be consistent for all of the cases. These were to visit the scene of the incidents in cases 1 and 5 (pesticides and train) i.e. the farm and the inland estuary, to go to the Cairngorm Chairlift Company to get an outline of the proposal (case 3), to the parents of the dead child (case 2) and finally to marine scientists who had authored the report on overfishing in the North Sea (case 4). It has emerged that the operational rules for cases 1 and 5 are similar as these are closely related types of story i.e. disaster/serious incident and require a special kind of reporting (see chapter 6). Cases 2, 3 and 4 initially require the journalists to contact the people involved in the scenarios in order to gain a starting point from which to build the line of enquiry in the report.

> The first thing I would do would be to go to the farm where there have been a few cases. I'd speak to the residents of the farm and presumably they'd have some more information perhaps from their doctor that would lead on to something else. [NNJ]

> The first thing I would do would be to go there. I would talk to the people who were ill. [SNJ]

> I'd talk to the Chairlift Company to find out what they were trying to achieve and find out what kind of assurances they were offering to limit the environmental impact of the development. [NTJ]

> The first person I'd talk to would be the general manager of Cairngorm Chairlift Company to say this is what we are proposing and why we are proposing it. [NRJ]

It has been suggested in the discussion about other categories that journalists tacitly contextualise the present assignment with a strategy used previously for similar events. It is now suggested that in using the operational rules to construct the news, this contextualising strategy is standard for the information procedures implemented at this point.

> It is quite a realistic [scenario] because I've done these stories in the past about, principally, organophosphates and the effects that they have, allegedly, had on others. To do that I've spoken to farmers themselves who have claimed that they've been affected and I invited them to explain the process by which they felt they'd been affected, the time scale, exactly what happened. [NTJ]

This journalist suggests that having completed a story on this issue previously he has a mental information strategy already prepared now. He knows how and where to start researching for the story, the people to contact, the angles which he has previously covered and, therefore, the different lines he will take this time. This tacit knowledge is analysed more fully below but it is worth mentioning here to introduce the discussion on journalistic strategies.

Journalistic strategies

Journalists frequently initiate their information strategies by visiting the scene of the incident (case 5) or interviewing the "victims" involved (case 2). One of the crucial procedures involved in investigating any story is to check the facts which have been given to reporters and this also involves verifying assertions which may appear in press releases.

Press releases are a common method of drawing potentially newsworthy items to the attention of journalists. They often come from environmental organisations and pressure groups and are biased towards their causes. These groups use the media to publicise and gain support for their political agendas (see chapter 1) and it is, therefore, necessary for news personnel to authenticate the statements included in these reports. Thus,

> ...you would need to get the basic facts. You need to start off at the scene. Go to the farmers themselves. Get basic information from emergency services. They are being treated, for what? And then when you've got that...I'd then go to the next stage which would be to try and speak to the people specifically who had been using the pesticide. [EC2(n)]

> There are various facts that are, here as, assertions but before I report them I need to establish whether or not they are true. I would try to speak to the doctors who could give me some sort of reportative analysis that there was a problem. I would speak to vets, definitely scientists, all the specialists to establish whether the animals died of natural or whether it has been caused by unnatural causes. [NTJ]

> Well assuming this came in as a press release from...it would probably come in as a tip off...but if it came in this form it would probably be from someone who had a vested interest in exposing it. Say it was from a trade union or from a "green" group. The first thing you would do would be to

check it out to see if it was true - to see if these people were really ill and if they were in hospital. [LNJ]

We would certainly need to talk to authorities on the matter to see if any link could be ascertained...but it would be an important thing to stress...that no-one could necessarily define it. We couldn't go ahead and say that this is what has caused it - a causal link - only a potential link exists between the two. [LNA1]

It was evident that all the journalists agreed on this point and stressed the fact that much of the information received in this manner is presented as claims which have to be validated by either the people involved or the appropriate authorities. These might be scientific experts, government sources, environmental specialists or technical advisors.

Examples of strategies

Although there are operational rules which are used in common by all journalists e.g. the use of the library for background information, going to the scene to identify "victims" or contacts, the journalistic strategies which reporters use are generally unique and distinct. Some may arrive at the same conclusions or in the case of a "disaster" the same facts may appear in a number of reports initially, but it is evident that the routes which journalists take when investigating the issue are different. This may be because they use their own subjective reasoning to identify and follow different lines or angles to the story. Further, contacts also direct journalists to specific lines or news lines.

The journalists outlined a variety of different ways to approach and define the story. For example, one reporter demonstrated how by contrasting the deaths in other areas with the death of the girl in Dundee, journalists can find a new angle on an "old" environmental issue.

You could look at deaths in other areas - there was an incident in London in 1992 ... about the smog and doctors have estimated since that there was an excess of something like about 50 deaths in the London area because of that. [EC2(n)]

One trend which emerged from the data suggests that the operational aspects of the journalistic process, like the evaluative and constructional/interpretive ones, are also used in combinations with other

103

rules by journalists. Furthermore, it is evident that the information strategy implemented for each story is not always clear cut and mapped out before the investigation begins.

> I must stress that as you go along...every time you do something it sparks off another chain of thought and you start to channel your enquiries. You'd phone the Forestry Commission, any farms or houses or shops or hotels along the route that might...say that this is going to ruin the tourist area...the tourist season anything like that. [NNJ]

It is only, therefore, when the story is underway that some angles will be presented. It is also apparent that there are a number of different story routes that can be taken and each time the construction of the end product will be unique. This is why no two journalists research or write the story in exactly the same way despite the fact that there are standard rules. However, journalists do visit similar places and interview many of the same contacts for stories. The operational aspects of the news process underline the subjective nature of journalism. Taking this into account some story angles present themselves in a more apparent way and these are covered in similar ways by most journalists. At the same time, there are some that are not so obvious. The latter are discovered and pursued by some journalists and not others. This is where coverage differs.

Cases 3 and 4 were stories that were tackled by the journalists in similar ways. For case 4, many of them decided to follow the story's main line first which was that fish stocks are becoming depleted in the North Sea and then the human interest angles which demonstrated the implications of this on the fishing industry and its workforce.

> I think that the main line of the story would be the fact that the fish are depleted and the fact that the fishing community up and down the coast of the North-East of Scotland are going to suffer massive unemployment. [LNA2]

> ...Your main report would have to be that fish stocks are depleting...why is this happening? You'd have your experts telling you this and your experts telling you that, whereas the human angle comes in the inside piece. The piece in which you might take a fisherman, hopefully, whose family has fished the North Sea for years, generations and you'd use him or her as a case study to illustrate the problems that this is creating for local fishermen. [ENJ]

For case 3 the story was a claim and counter claim which is straightforward to cover as the journalists simply report the comments of each side, balancing the argument. The obvious or overt lines which appeared are discussed below and these are the ones which most journalists admitted to taking,

> ...the line that I would probably take would be that conservationists are banding together to try to prevent a new ski development in the Highlands and then bring up in the next paragraph, the amount of jobs that would be created and that type of thing. [LNA2]

> I'd speak to the local Save the Cairngorms Campaign to find out exactly what their reservations were, how they justify these concerns, how great their fears were, how substantial would be the damage to the landscape and the habitat and to the wildlife...I'd also want to find out if there was a presumption against planning extension in the local property area. I'd find another area akin to this and look at that and at the impact there was and how many extra people were attracted, what the pros and cons of that were. [NTJ]

Case 3 included an outline of the proposal by the Cairngorm Chairlift Company and to investigate the opposition to this development by environmental groups. Other lines demonstrated the implications for tourism and for the economy of the local area.

Case 5, which, in the discussion of the other categories, has been identified as being distinct from the other cases, has again been considered separately. It has already been established that "disaster" reporting is different from routine coverage of issues. Once again, however, the journalists tended to approach the issue from similar angles. This is because in these situations there are greater demands on reporters to communicate certain standard strands of information. These were firstly, what had happened and why it had happened and secondly the environmentalists' points of view.

The journalists divided the coverage into (a) the description of incident and (b) the effects on society and the environment. This was prioritised in an order that is dictated by extra-personal factors such as the audience or readership (discussed in chapter 8).

> There would be any number of different aspects to it - the environmental aspect of the birds that are affected and the aquatic life, the health aspects - whether people are affected by it, you know streaming eyes, skin

complaints. There would be the...whether the drinking water was affected and then all the other aspects - how it happened, what are they doing to clean it up, whether they were spraying chemicals, chemical dispersants. The [journalists] go into everything - how old the train was, the last time it was maintained, whether trains like this had had accidents before. What were they doing immediately to ensure that other trains carrying fuel didn't crash....how Scotrail were responsible....[LNJ]

It is an easy story to cover because it's a disaster. It gets more complicated on day two or three where you get issues like should this have been going by road or rail. What were the safety precautions, has there been a lack of investment in the safety side of it. You would start to tease out those kinds of angles. You would be looking at some of the seals that had hopefully been rescued and talk to the RSPB but dead straightforward. [EC(b)]

The fact that this type of incident is a rare occurrence has a bearing on how the information strategy is formulated.

The ways, in which journalists formulate their information strategies with a view to researching the issue, are complex. In some stories, angles/lines present themselves with clarity, in others they do not. A mixture of operational rules exist at this stage in the process. There are those which are used in common by reporters such as visiting the scene or interviewing the "victims" first, and there are those which illustrate the diversity and distinction of journalistic operational rules, for example, the selection of different "experts" and angles to view the situation from.

Information gathering

Information is gathered, by journalists, from a variety of sources. These include among other things personal contacts, electronic databases and now the internet. In each situation i.e. for each story, reporters establish the basic facts first. This may mean describing the scene of a disaster e.g. case 5 or reporting the main issue e.g. that an eight year old girl has died (case 2). It is only after this has been accomplished that reporters can allow the coverage to diversify by following other angles and related developments e.g. the implications of oil pollution on the eiderduck population or the debate about too many cars being allowed in inner city areas. At each stage in researching a story, journalists are making decisions. These decisions include who to contact, who to interview for

106

comment, how to balance the selection of these contacts, and, which databases to search. Journalism is by nature a decision-based profession but it is in teasing out the operational rules which reporters use to locate, retrieve and gather information that this becomes more apparent.

Journalists' self tests

Environment correspondents often set up self-initiated tests, for example to test for air pollution. These journalists admitted to hiring equipment to gauge the air pollution levels in order to include extra results in their reports. The purpose was, in some cases, to pad out the story or in others to give the issue a new line. Both broadcast and newspaper correspondents did this,

> ...in fact you could do [it yourself]...newspapers these days can hire pollution monitoring equipment and set up our own test. This happens a lot, especially in local papers. You can hire it for £10-15 and they stick it in the street and say that a test shows X amount of pollution. [EC2(n)]

> If there is no-one actually measuring pollution in the street where this girl lived...we can set that up ourselves. Other television programmes have won awards for that so it's not entirely original but it's still quite a good thing to do if no-one else is doing that kind of research and there are quite reasonable ways of doing that these days. [EC(b)]

Consequently, it may be suggested that although, in theory, this might seem like a good idea i.e. a practical way to gather data to substantiate a news report, in practice, it begs the question, what training do journalists receive in the interpretation of scientific evidence? It has already been established that reporters in Britain do not receive tuition in scientific reporting on academic courses (follow-up interview with LNJ). This forces us to consider the amount of expertise journalists can use to evaluate the results of these tests and therefore what conclusions can be drawn about an issue such as traffic density and air pollution in inner cities. These interpretive implications raise serious questions not only about the validity of the scientific information which journalists include but also about the self perceptions which environment correspondents have about their role and ability as subject specialists. What prompts journalists, specifically specialist correspondents, to make this kind of decision? One possibility is related to the pragmatics of the news process. If a story has to be "padded out" to fit a particular news hole or space in

107

the schedule, the data gathered from this test can be used to fill in the background information to a news report. This is a decision that is based on the requirements of the editorial norms.

Sources

Information sources are vital to the journalist, providing the necessary raw material for the news construction process. It has already been established that Scottish journalists rely on the library as an information depository and now have access to a variety of electronic sources e.g. the internet. The library generally provides a valuable support service to journalists in Scotland. Indeed, the library support in the larger Scottish media institutions e.g. BBC Scotland and *The Herald*, may be described as being the vital core of the information network within these organisations.

The secondary stage of the model describes the news process within a particular reporting context and this cross-section shows the sources reporters use and indicates both human and impersonal (see Figure 10, points B and C).

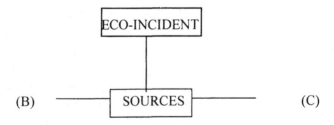

Figure 10 Excerpt from Secondary Stage of Model

At the time of this research, journalists did not receive training in electronic information retrieval or the availability of electronic sources and this was thought to be a reason as to why reliance is placed on "human" sources rather than on impersonal ones. These human sources include the subject specialists (mainly scientific and environmental) to whom journalists refer for specific types of information.

A number of the journalists were of the opinion that the benefits of electronic information sources outweigh the disadvantages. The sample was divided on this issue into those who were unclear about the usefulness of electronic retrieval tools and those who were frustrated due to the fact they were denied use of them (at the time of this research). Those journalists who were familiar with this type of information technology discussed it as follows,

> ...these days you can get a fair amount of information from computerised library systems...which give you access to large amounts of journalists and newspapers as well. We'd key in "pesticides" and see what comes out on a story and it's one you don't have much expertise in. [EC2(n)]

> We don't unfortunately use electronic sources of information. Not because we don't want to but because we don't have access. The height of the electronics we have...is a system which is linked up to Mercury... our stuff goes down into electronic mail boxes and everything we do is retained on that system...so we can go back and look at our own stuff. So if we'd done a story about rape seed oil in the past and we were doing one now, we'd look it up. So that is an electronic source. It's a small-scale electronic library. Ideally if we were up and running, we'd have PROFILE but that's just a question of resources. [LNA1]

This last journalist suggests that his organisation uses a small, self-contained, electronic depository. This is used by staff to search for stories written previously on a relevant and current topic by themselves i.e. personnel at the agency. This begs the question of information recycling as proposed by the communication model which occurs when newspaper articles are divided into cuttings which are thematically arranged in the library or are transposed onto electronic format and to which journalists refer back in order to retrieve background information for their current articles. This is discussed more fully below.

Several of the journalists indicated that they either used or desired to make use of *FT PROFILE* an online information service which contains international news and current affairs files, including newspapers like *The Daily* and *Sunday Telegraph*, *The Herald* and *The Observer*. Many of these are full text, meaning that the files are complete transcripts of the newspapers. None of the journalists, at the time, were able to get personal access to *PROFILE* and had to use the library staff as intermediaries.

...[Checking] something like [Lurchers' Gully] you probably won't need to get the library staff to do it for you. I could do that through our own library system as I have access to it. I wouldn't need to go into FT Profile for it. We have our own files on Lurcher's Gully. I can't do a FT PROFILE search from here. I can only look through what's in our own library system. We can't get into other newspapers' files so that's why the library staff has to do it for us. [EC1(n)]

It is a resource which is becoming more widely used in the larger, British national newspapers and broadcast organisations but which was relatively unknown to journalists north of the border (at the time of this research). It is known, now, that most Scottish journalists have access to the internet and can use FT PROFILE.

Library context

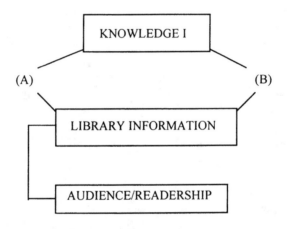

Figure 11 Excerpt from Preliminary Stage of Model

The cross-section of the preliminary model describes the "internal cycle" discussed below.

The end product i.e. the news is filed in the library for future reference. Newspapers are not kept in their entirety but are dissected into subjects. This selection process might be seen to be influencing future news construction due to the "recycling" of information which allows journalists to refer to each other's work. How reasonable is it to assume that the same information is therefore perpetuated through this internal information cycle? The problem is perhaps not wholly concerned simply with the information itself but rather with the journalists' information retrieval strategies. For example, reporters looking for material on the Braer for background to an article on another oil spill, can influence the construction of their story by referring to the same particular journalists' work. More specifically, one journalist might persist in underestimating the disastrous proportions of a nuclear accident like Chernobyl even when this type of incident deserves a greater amount of coverage. If this material is retrieved at a later date as background when this incident has been forgotten this could influence future news construction by perpetuating a myth. It can also be dependent on how selective or comprehensive the information strategy is. If, for example, reporters look at the earlier coverage of the Braer which tried to demonstrate how irrevocable the damage to Shetland's environment was as opposed to the later news stories which reversed the preliminary coverage, then this selection will influence the construction of the news story. Journalists do consult library files for previous stories that have been written on the issue. This is not only to check the angles that have been covered, but also to check facts (these are supposed to be checked by an independent source also) and to identify experts or interviewees who were presumably press-friendly at that time.

> It will cause a film all over the surface of the sea so this could be very dodgy but we'd look for our fuel expert...probably go back to the cuttings a bit and find out who was talking at the time of the Braer. That's from the library - go to the newspaper cuttings under "oil pollution" and see which names come out of the hat. [EC2(n)]

> ...Other asthma sufferers have died obviously - how could they have claimed that the death was from air pollution - I don't know I'd have to check that with our library...to see if they'd come across anything before. I wouldn't want to, for example, repeat a story which had been done before at some other time, perhaps several weeks or months beforehand, unless it was to demonstrate a claim or a growing trend or to develop the issue into a feature rather than a simple report of the events. [NTJ]

Journalists do consult the library of old newspaper cuttings to check for angles or stories previously completed on a particular issue. Further, journalists also re-use information strategies to research the story and often the information which has already been mediated (KNOWLEDGE

II) is redisseminated through the new product.

Contacts

This sentiment is echoed by some of the other journalists and practitioners turned academics such as, Harris (1987), Boyd (1990) and Hausman (1991). The fact that journalism is so decision-based is further underlined by the strategies involved in selecting contacts. The selection of interviewees for comment is carried out in similar ways when journalists are reporting on the same story. When reporting on environmental issues, the contacts to which journalists turn are mainly scientific. Among the other groups of people targeted by reporters are those drawn from government, industry and technical spheres. "Victims" are often interviewed by journalists first because they can be at the centre of the story - the key characters. These are people who are not usually specialists (experts) and who are interviewed by journalists for comment in a different capacity to that of the other contacts to whom they turn. The "victims" are the actors who provide the human face of the issue and allow the audience a point of interaction with the issue. They are the people with whom the journalists make the first point of contact, for example the ill workers in case 1, the parents of the dead child in case 2 and, if case 5 had had any casualties, the injured parties would take precedence over the details about the train. The contact groups are best illustrated in the following diagram.

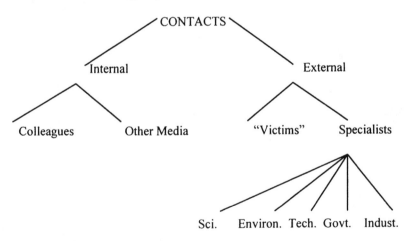

Figure 12 Diagram of Journalistic Contacts

Internal contacts

It has already been established that the media monitor each other constantly i.e. broadcasters scrutinise the papers and newspapers survey the news via TV and radio. This is in part a consequence of differences in the logistics of the media. There is a "recycling" of information due to this continual referral procedure that takes place within the news process. This has been characterised by the secondary stage of the model.

> They are probably likely to have called a press conference or maybe the fishing correspondent from the Press and Journal goes on and says I believe you are doing something and they say "yes - we are just about to complete the study. We know what it is all about" and then we think it is a good story and we might pick up on it from another outlet...It may be that Grampian or the newspaper would run with it first and the beauty of what we do is that people will not be watching the TV. [LRJ]

> One of the things you probably do a lot on these stories - you are in the office and you watch television, listen to the radio and read the evening papers. [NNJ]

It was suggested that radio is probably the fastest type of media in its ability to broadcast breaking news first (e.g. this was the medium which initially carried the Braer story). However, an important point worthy of due consideration is that the speed with which the news is constructed and disseminated depends on newsworthiness of the incident. The fact that the Braer ran aground off the coast of Shetland, makes the incident newsworthy to the Scottish media as a whole, but also makes the grounding more relevant to Shetland's media.

Scientific contacts (experts specific to areas of scientific arena other than the environment)

Many media organisations have policies that stipulate what journalists should or should not do. These can be ethical issues or logistical issues for example who to contact or refer to. For example,

> ...these full time journalists will be supplemented by specialists adding their own skill and expertise in such areas as national and local politics, farming, industry and commerce, energy, fishing, sport, economics, international affairs and legal matters. This network of experts,

continually reviewed and updated, will be used on a regular basis. [Grampian Television, 1991]

The above is an excerpt from the proposal put forward by Grampian Television for their licence renewal in 1992 and reinforces the importance of experts in the operational part of the news process, as determined by the organisation.

It was evident both from interviews with journalists and also from interviews with scientific specialists that each group views the other from a different perspective. Both have very different professional ideals so it is not surprising that disagreements arise between the two (see chapter 3).

It is argued that the relationship between the scientist and the media influences the operational aspects of the news process. The journalist's perception of the scientific expert is of a contact who will add credence to the news report and therefore to the reality being emulated.

Wilkinson and Waterton's (1991, p53-56) report into the public's attitude to the environment in Scotland states that the audience looks for guidance, in environmental and scientific issues, to the media, as this is the main source of available information (see also chapter 1). The media contacts scientific experts to refer to for their knowledge and expertise. It is the opinion of experts and journalists alike that the media require scientists to give their stories authenticity and validity.

Scientific or environmental information is pluralistic and complex. It is highly technical in nature and consequently it is difficult for the lay person i.e. individual without a background knowledge of the subjects and their terminology, to understand. Without this understanding it is impossible for the lay person to use and apply the information effectively.

Journalists act as intermediaries between the environmental information and the wider social community. The relationship between journalists and scientific specialists influences the type of information journalists retrieve. Further, the scientist acts as an intermediary between the environmental information and the journalists. The scientific expert interprets the information by explaining technical concepts to the non-expert (journalist). Similarly, the journalist interprets the scientific information for the lay person. Hence, the fact that information changes as it is retrieved, interpreted, and disseminated, is underlined.

The journalists acknowledged that they are aware of the problems associated with the communication of science (see chapter 8).

People are unlikely to go back and read something four times to understand it - so what we would probably do is go and ask a scientist who is an expert in the area to try and explain it in layman's terms. So rather than me misinterpret it - I would rather ask the scientists themselves to put it into simple terms. [EC1(n)]

I'd probably want to speak to individual scientists because you've got...all this information that I'd want explained. You know from the point of view of transposing it into reasonable, readable newscopy. I'd have to be able to understand it myself first. So rather than go through a medium of a press officer I'd probably want to speak to the scientist himself, so that he could explain what all these chemicals are, what their uses are, how dangerous they are and...what are the possibilities that these are the causes of the illness. [LNJ]

I would phone the universities' press offices and try to get them to put me on to someone who could explain all this...make it so that I can understand it , so that I can write about it. [NNJ]

Scientists are high on the list of source priorities for journalists to contact in, for example, cases 1, 4 and 5. Cases 2 and 3 would be approached differently in that the most important initial contacts are the parents of the child and the chairlift company. However, in cases 2 and 3, the scientific specialists would be likely to be the second priority.

...Once you have spoken to the people at the scene...if they'll speak to you. The next step would be to go to the institutions...scientists, in this case, Aberdeen University and The Robert Gordon University scientists. [EC2(N), case 1]

The scientist would give us the break down of what these chemicals do and if people were exposed to them what their symptoms would be. We'd also have to speak to people who knew how many of these chemicals were used in this particular case and how exposed the workers were. [LNJ, case 1]

It has already been established that during a "disaster" type situation, the type of coverage changes. It has been argued that journalists use a method of contextualisation where they tacitly refer to a template of the specific types of rules of reporting e.g. the Braer. Within the operational category there is also evidence to suggest that this type of scenario has a particular format. The "disaster" situation is much more

115

highly pressurised in that the news process develops more rapidly and to a greater extent than usual. A new set of rules take precedence. In this setting journalists do not have to seek out contacts as often as during other types of story. Environmental and scientific experts converge on the scene to take part in press conferences which are arranged more frequently than in other types of reporting. It is normal in these settings for experts to seek journalists out rather than the other way about.

> Any zoologists or ecologists - anybody you could contact, but these people would probably be around the scene. You wouldn't need to chase them. [NNJ]

One of the operational rules that emerged from this work was that journalists do depend on their colleagues for the identification of appropriate contacts. It was very evident that during this type of story (case 5) reporters are much more dependent on each other.

> You would need someone who is a medical expert who could explain the medical aspects. Out of all these things would hopefully come other contacts. I'd also be speaking to my colleagues as I do all the time - like the Agency (North Scot), who I know you have spoken to...and *The Record* and *The Scotsman*. We'd all exchange notes to some degree to find out whom they've spoken to - who's the best to speak to. [NNJ1]

> There would be a lot of other journalists and you would ask them where they'd been and would swop contacts...we all help each other in that situation, particularly in the branch offices because we all know each other pretty well and one man can't do everything...so you avoid unnecessary work basically. [NNJ2]

Journalists have pools of contacts i.e. personal sources which are used repeatedly because of their "press friendly" attitude. These "key" contacts exist in all subjects but individuals can be transferred across the disciplines when needed to validate or comment on an issue in a related field. There are definite implications inherent in this action. It may be seen that news is defined in part by the relationship between the journalist and the scientific specialists (experts). The journalist often uses the same contacts for certain kinds of information. It can be argued, therefore, that the selection process reinforces the construction of the news product, for by choosing the same contacts repeatedly the same type of comment is being perpetuated.

One journalist made this very clear by emphasising that journalists talk to each other about their assignments constantly and refer to each other for specialist contacts. He also stated that doing this is a way of saving time that is a pragmatic factor that all journalists have to take account of.

Environmental contacts

Specialist reporters and more experienced senior journalists have a much clearer idea as to the contacts that are available and appropriate, particularly in the environmental and scientific fields. They can instantly focus on a number of people whom they term as "press friendly" i.e. people who give comment readily.

> I'd probably...speak to a couple of environmental experts in the field. I know that WWF has got an expert on fishing stocks...so I would speak to them and they would warn me of the dangers and would put forward their ideas as to what should be done. A lot of the environmental groups will have their own strategies/plans for what should be done and this is what they would be lobbying the government to do. [EC1(n)]

The specialist reporters were very likely to use the names of real contacts as opposed to their generic occupation titles. For example, "Drennen Watson" as opposed to "a representative of the Save the Cairngorms Campaign".

> Dick Balharry of the Scottish Natural Heritage is always a good moderate [voice] in the sense that he very well understands the need for development and improving the tourism and all the rest of it. Dave Morris of the Ramblers is good but gives a rather extreme anti-view and [he is] someone who also went through the Lurcher's Gully inquiry and remembers that pretty intimately. There's no shortage of people to go to, the difficulty is coming to any firm conclusion. [EC2(n)]

> You tend to get to know who the main experts are in the field and particularly with the environmental movement - RSPB, WWF who are very well respected in that field - so I would speak to the people in the marine lab. [EC1(n)]

Journalists use a tacit form of contextualisation when constructing the news and this is true also of the operational category of rules. When talking about environmental contacts one journalist provided a further example of this,

> ...you are thinking on your feet all the time. It is like the Braer where you are running about like a nutcase trying to pull it all together. But people were seeking you out at the Braer like Greenpeace. They're telling you "we're having a press conference, will you come to that". [NNJ]

The journalists indicated how a new environmental contact was selected. This was accomplished either through an already existing, "press friendly" contact or by phoning the university or conservation body.

> You've got the stuff in the office and you would have your contacts book. You'd phone one that you knew was involved in the environment - you could phone Greenpeace and they'd tell you the man you want to speak to and on it goes. You don't have to search for them. You don't have to have a huge bank of names in your mind. [NNJ]

Journalists approach different groups of contacts in particular ways. They have specific strategies for handling them. Practitioners were quick to point out that because groups use the media to get their point of view across to the audience, they have to be aware of the hidden political agendas which are often embedded in promotional documentation (press releases). This knowledge which journalists possess is not tacit and journalists develop this skill as they acquire experience. During the discussion of case 1, a specialist journalist indicated that Greenpeace and Friends of the Earth are the two pressure groups which are at the forefront of pesticide research and that they would almost certainly provide files of information for the report. However it was made clear that the reporter might not necessarily interview the scientists at either Friends of the Earth or Greenpeace for the story.

> It's probably more likely that finally Friends of the Earth and Greenpeace's names will not appear on the report. But they are a very useful point of contact...we have a kind of understanding and they supply me with information but don't expect as a matter of course to have a name check. [EC2(n)]

Pressure groups like these, then, do not gain explicit publicity but do manage to communicate their environmental message to the audience.

Medical experts were appropriate for cases 1 and 2. Environmental and political contacts were relevant for cases 3, 4, and 5. Therefore, it is the experts most relevant for the story who will be contacted by journalists. It is this relevancy which journalists look for when scanning incoming information.

> Doctors, physicians, politicians...ask if there has been an increase in asthma. Asthma is one of the few diseases which is dramatically increasing, so you could to a background piece looking at the growing incidents with asthmatics. I would go to the British Lung Foundation and say, "look what do you think about this?" and they would say, "...there is a strong link between traffic and asthma" but they'll also tell you that it's not the only link. We'd go to doctors and the Department of Transport. [EC2(n)]

This journalist talks about his information strategy where he is going to start looking for information, the contacts he is going to use and the reasoning which he is applying to continue and advance the search.

In some cases, the journalists stated that they would approach political contacts whether it be at government, regional or local level. For example,

> I'd speak to the Scottish Office fisheries experts. I'd probably speak directly to the press office and they would probably come back at you with comments from them. Very rarely at the Scottish Office do you get through to the experts themselves. They are quite often heavily screened. [EC1(n)]

Journalists are aware and resigned to the fact that often the comments from government organisations are sanitised and disseminated for the media's benefit through the political mechanism. This problem is alleviated when they talk to a range of contacts from different organisations thereby balancing the news report (see chapter 6).

Two specific conclusions about the types of specialists (experts) which journalists refer to can be drawn. Many of the journalists related long lists of contacts which were presented in no particular order but occurred just as the reporters thought of them at random. Therefore, trying to make sense of the ways in which journalists logically select contacts forces the author to draw this conclusion. Reporters digest the information given to them and in formulating their research strategies, contacts that are easily available, "press friendly", relevant to the issue etc. are targeted. Further, and more importantly, the repeated selection of certain scientific specialists (experts) because of their accessibility has a definite, constructional influence on the formation of the news product. Further, the pragmatics of the situation (see below), forces the journalists to operate under great pressure (deadlines) and this undoubtedly influences the contact selection and indeed the whole information research process.

Influence of extrapersonal perceptions

The evaluative and contructional/interpretive categories indicate that the journalist is profoundly influenced by the audience/readership. This influence is less direct within the operational category. It is argued that the news hierarchy is dictated, to a greater or lesser extent, by the journalist's perceptions of the needs and interests of the audience. For example, in case 5, the approach to the story is prioritised using evaluative rules in that a chronology of facts is ordered first, followed by the "disaster" as it affects the humans and then the "disaster" as it affects the environment. This demonstrates that each rule category exists in combination with the other two.

The audience/readership does have an effect in that it may be seen to influence to some extent the information strategies which journalists use in covering environmental issues. Specifically, this refers to the ways in which journalists select people to interview. For example in case 1, the respondents chose to interview a large number of farmers, agriculture experts and farming union officials. This is not unusual in that the issue surrounds a farming incident but several respondents admitted that this line was taken because a great proportion of the readership or audience were involved in the farming industry.

> ...We have got a big farming readership in the North East and presumably they would be more familiar with these pesticides. I mean we also.... purely from the point of view of not alienating the readership as well...you know... we'd probably play reasonably safe with this. We'd go to the NFU...the farming union and we'd go to the farm itself. We'd want to know specifically how far we could go in suggesting that pesticides were the cause of the illness...because we've got a lot of farmers that read the

paper. We would want to make sure that we could make the link. [LNJ]

Journalists do not simply report news. As they report news and make decisions about how to structure it, they are influenced by a number of factors (see chapter 4) such as organisational and editorial demands, the advertisers, and the audience but also by their own perceptions of the audience or readership.

> I'd have to speak to the scientists and so forth to find out what's causing it...newspaper readers would be more concerned with how the people are, what their symptoms are and...they'd only broadly be interested in what specifically caused it. [LNJ]

Pragmatic factors of information gathering

As with all the other categories, the operational one also is bound by the constraints of pragmatics. The journalists admitted to following a "take what you can get" policy, indicating that they start with an idea of who they would like to interview but realistically acknowledging that their contacts must be the people who can be reached at the time and who are willing to converse with the media.

> In the end you are starting with a kind of wish list. You're looking for a farmer, you are looking for someone who has been ill, you're looking for someone who has been campaigning locally on this kind of issue...You are hoping for a local doctor or a local environmental health officer and you are hoping for a scientist...with a bit of back up information from one of the pressure groups. In the end you would probably only get three of those and that would be enough but that is the list you would start with. You narrow it down by finding out who is available and who's going to talk, who can get to a studio or who is available when you turn up in the area with a camera crew. [EC(b)]

> You're not going to phone [the second] if you get through to the first one...you're not going to go to all the sources. If you got a good quote the first time then you're going to drop the rest of them. [NNJ]

In the end, journalists admit that because they are bound by the constraints of time in producing the news, they do not follow up an unending supply of contacts and interviewees and that on receiving the appropriate type of comment from a selection of people will stop

121

searching for further contacts. Continuing in this vein, then, reporters will not spend a great deal of time wading through background e.g. scientific information, rather they will go to an expert or specialist and ask for a synopsis of the material in layman's terms. This is partly because they need to communicate the information to a lay audience/readership and partly because of the short amount of time available to them in the news construction process.

> I don't think we'd contact the National Asthma Campaign. The nature of the news business is so quick, we would be relying on the medical school to make that connection between asthma and death and traffic problems. [LTJ]

> [I might sift through this stuff]...it depends. You'd flick through it very, very quickly and try and work out what was relevant or maybe get them to fax you two or three pages. It's all kind of deciding as you go along. [NNJ]

Although journalists have been accused of covering scientific issues in a superficial way, it must be acknowledged that the reporting of this type of complex information precludes the non-scientist from comprehensively summarising the main arguments of the issue quickly and wholly. One of the main journalistic skills which reporters have to learn quickly is the ability to read and amass information or to absorb information quickly and accurately. This type of task becomes more difficult when the information is as complex and diverse as the type that emanates from the environmental or scientific disciplines.

There are differences too between the different strands of the media. Television and radio news is, on the whole, much shorter and more rapidly put together than newspaper stories where there is greater scope for coverage and a longer time to assemble it. The tertiary model describes these concepts.

Tertiary stage of model

The discussion in this chapter has shown that the operational category is one which is quite distinct from the others but which is still important in the intertextuality of the news process. This category again reinforces and demonstrates how decision-based journalism is as a profession. Journalists' information strategy rules can be divided into two parts. How journalists approach the issue in an operational sense i.e. what lines are going to be taken in the search strategy and the information gathering routines i.e. sources to contact.

The tertiary stage of the model (see following page) shows the integration of the evaluative and operational rules by describing concepts such as the ways journalists approach the issue by identifying particular angles from which they can follow a story. They can do this by revealing links between concepts developing within the issue e.g. in case 1, the pesticides and human illness or in case 2 the atmospheric pollution and the death of the asthmatic child. These links cannot be implied unless they have been verified by the relevant authoritative figure e.g. scientists or medical research workers. If the journalist does state a causal link between factors such as these and there is a lack of evidence to support the claim, then, he or she is guilty of negating their role of responsibility to the public (see sources, chapter 4).

The information gathering routines of the journalist are non-tacit in that they are aware of the types of sources that can be accessed and more specifically who they can contact in the relevant fields for comment. These sources can be divided into two parts - human and impersonal. The sources at this stage are described in greater detail than in comparison with the preliminary and secondary stages of the model. These human contacts are, for example, subject specialists (experts) who may be scientific or environmental, or non-specialists like politicians, technical personnel. Internal contacts also fall into this category. These may be colleagues within the newsrooom who often provide information easily and quickly (a sharing of resources) or colleagues outwith the newsroom who work in other areas of the media. When journalists monitor other media they may not contact colleagues personally. This is often a method that involves keeping up to date with current events as they happen. It is, therefore, an information strategy also. Impersonal sources are, as the model suggests, mainly institutional e.g. the library or information office at the environmental interest group. These institutions provide the majority of the technical information which journalists may use to construct their articles with.

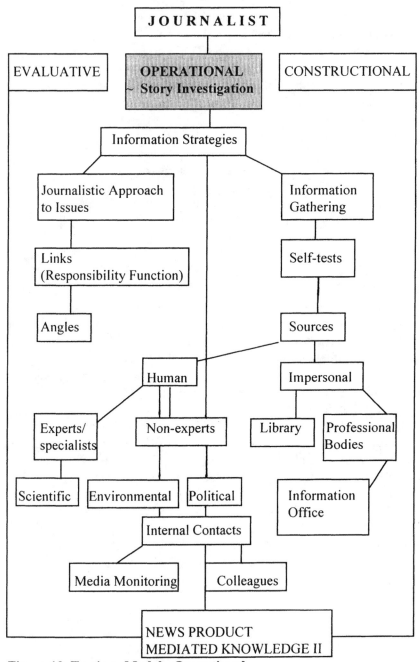

Figure 13 Tertiary Model: Operational

The operational category is decision-based and contains rules that focus on the journalistic information strategies inherent in the news process. These strategies include, the identification of news angles, the selection of contacts to interview, the retrieval of information from a variety of sources e.g. libraries, scientific specialists and journalist colleagues. There are implications, in the repetition of information, for the construction of the end product due to the fact that journalists' information gathering strategies are limited in comprehensiveness and information is "recycled" when the news copy is circulated back into the library for future reference.

Furthermore, the journalist is influenced in his/her operations by images of the intended audience or readership e.g. in case 1 where particular care is taken to allow the farmers and farming experts a voice. In addition to this the journalist is directed by the perceptions he/she holds of the powers of comprehension possessed by the audience. This idea is explored in greater detail in the next chapter (constructional/interpretive). The language and semantic structures that reporters use are dependent on the types of paper or broadcast medium being supplied with copy. Complex terminology is diluted and simplified by journalists.

8 Constructional/Interpretive Rules

To say that news reports present a mythic, narrative system is to say that it describes signs (actions and events) that are presented through a series of cultural filters which include values of the reporting and reading culture. News reportage thus takes the raw events of our world and places them in a unifying context, a translation that renders them comprehensible and safe to readers or viewers, who can disregard that system of presentation just as readers of this passage do not stop to think of the degree to which the language (English) and style (academic-narrative) that order these words as I write also define and limit my mode of presentation. (Koch, 1990, p21)

The constructional and interpretive categories are interlinked and they are complementary to each other. This chapter discusses both these types of rules.

Tiffen (1989) discusses the format of news in relation to organisational production and states,

...the most basic format consideration which is shared by all news media is that news only becomes suitable when it is transformed into a story...every story must always include a lead, a narrative and a closer. Leads which are also "hookers" designed to attract audience attention, raise a moral issue, or question a common expectation (or stereotype)... The narrative illustrates the lead...the closer assesses the significance of the original highlight, offers a momentary resolution to the issue or debunks or reaffirms the expectation. This story format, therefore, creates or reinforces symbols to make it possible for the news to become a morality play. (Tiffen, 1989, p64)

He suggests that the story format which journalists use is a formula and that if a story differs from this pattern it is less likely to be accepted by the news editor. Several of the journalists who were interviewed supported this argument. The following comment is from the discussion of case 1.

126

...Like any job, journalism is about trying to establish a formula and so there would be a particular formula which would be followed for this type of story. [LNJ]

The construction of news is repeated in formulas. These are routinised procedures or rules that are shaped by (among others) various factors like the organisational and editorial cultures of the institution and the training received at colleges or on site. Willis (1991) underlines this idea and states that through the process of mastering a number of journalistic skills, a composite view of reality will be gained. He talks about a pseudo-world perpetuated by the state media where if this media skews the interpretation of an event, audience response will be influenced and this in turn will affect actions in the real world (Willis, 1991, p6).

The constructional rules are concerned with the writing, editing and presentation of the news story. These, like the operational rules, refer to the structuring of the news. The interpretive rules are implicit in the ways in which information is codified and simplified for the end user i.e. the audience/readership. These, together with the evaluative rules, refer to the selection (often termed by journalism textbooks as news gathering) and reduction of news.

This chapter deals with certain themes that have emerged from the discovery of both types of rules, for example, the difficulties attached to the communication of science, the journalist as an intellectual filter for the audience, and the journalist's perceptions of the audience.

The constructional rules include fact ordering i.e. the ways in which facts are assembled in a newsworthy priority. This underlines the point that the categories in the typology used by journalists complement each other. The journalists indicated that facts are not always arranged in a chronological order but are prioritised according to their news value. The following comments come from the discussion of case 1.

...Writing it up is a rather difficult question to answer because this is just a scenario...not the actual story. If the story is on a pesticide...people have been exposed to this pesticide and that it had caused illness...then the story is a simple one. It's simple in the sense that "X" number of people have become ill, having been exposed to a pesticide...you then, have to detail what the symptoms are, how these people were exposed, were they using the pesticide correctly, should they have been using protective clothing, what is the pesticide.... [EC2(n)]

When I am first presented with information like that, I will write a story to present the facts to people. So this has happened and this has happened, two animals have been found dead, several people are taken ill, no clear link has been established. Scientists from Aberdeen University have been called in to investigate. The cases have been reported in X, Y, and Z. That tells people the story. We will run it for maybe two bulletins and then we are looking...from that moment we start running it...we are looking forward and thinking how can we develop it across the day. [LRJ]

The way in which practitioners write is constrained by certain parameters (discussed below) like the audience for whom the news is intended or the news values of the organisation. In effect, this underlines the fact that the news is a constructed entity. It is not a natural phenomenon.

Everybody has a structure within which they write the story...nobody just reports the facts...you know yourself that the process of reporting the facts involves ordering the facts. If you are asking if there is a framework within which we are told we should assemble these facts then the answer is no...we have to quote facts as facts and assertions as such and we don't make assertions ourselves and we don't draw conclusions, unless we work in a specific field where we might be invited to explain some of the background but as a non-specialist I would simply be reporting the facts on what had happened. [NBJ1]

It is possible to put a spin on a story when the journalists assemble the facts into a particular order and it apparently happens quite frequently in some organisations. Some of the journalists talked about this when discussing how they would construct the news story.

The claims which they use in the story are what they believe to have happened...The order in which I choose to assemble the facts, I could put a spin on the story. I wouldn't because again that would be unprofessional and unethical. I would try and make it as straight as I could. [NBJ1]

I think that even the dullest paper puts a spin on the way it reports news. It makes stories more interesting if you jack them up. It kind of permeates the whole process of reporting - the ordinary reporter is working to me and I'm working to the news editor who is working to the editor. At every stage in the process the story is being jacked up more and more because the reporter wants to be seen to be doing his job and so he sells you the story at a higher pitch than it warrants. Then I've got to be seen to have a bank of reasonable news stories for the statement so when the news editor asks me what I've got, I jack the story up even further. I think that's probably unavoidable. It's not a particularly justifiable phenomenon but it happens. [LNJ]

In some news organisations, then, the basic factual information is dressed up with drama to make it more acceptable at higher levels in the editorial chain. Certain facts are given more emphasis than others i.e. they are ordered in a particular way to give the story greater impact. This is exemplified by the tertiary model, below and further is discussed in greater detail in this chapter.

Tertiary stage of model

The whole tertiary level of the model is a statement describing the integration of the different types of rules elicited from the respondents' coded data. The relationship between the evaluative, operational and editorial rules has been evident from the previous chapter. This chapter seeks to describe the interaction of all the categories with the addition of the final chronological component in the news process, the constructional category.

This is concerned with the writing of the story. It is the transformation of the raw material ie the information is put into an organised format through the writing process and the editing process. The interpretive rules that are always implicit in the constructional category, are embedded in the writing process. Besides having the more obvious rules and constructional procedures like the dramatic writing styles that are linked to the negativity aspect of the evaluative category, the journalist acts as an intellectual filter. This role is assumed when the journalist performs the task of reducing complex, scientific information for stories. This is a subjective emphasis on the selection of information for news reports because journalists make conscious decisions as to what to accept and what to reject. It is in this way that the journalist acts as a filter when producing the news. In reducing the complexity of this type of environmental or scientific information, the journalist places new meanings on the information, thus, creating a new information level (as described by the preliminary stage of the model). This reduction process is also a subjective one because it has been revealed that the journalist uses him/herself as a yardstick against which the relevant level of scientific information can be estimated. This is a tacit rule which

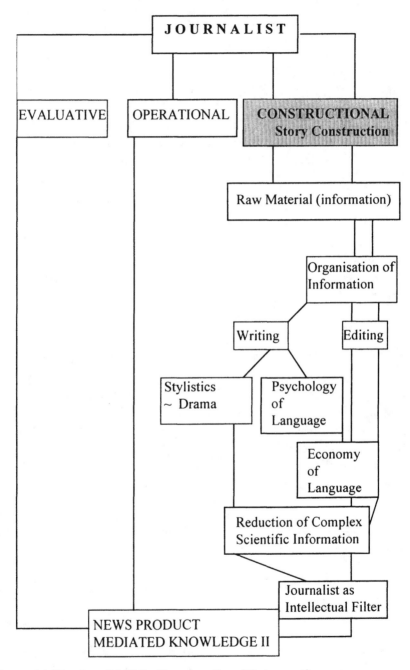

Figure 14 Tertiary Model: Constructional/Interpretive

130

journalists implement with an image of the intended audience in mind. It is a function described previously by the secondary stage of the model (see chapter 3). The reduction of complex information is, however, also a device to economise on language i.e. an editing technique. A key aim in journalism is to communicate the facts of a story, using simple terminology as succinctly and rapidly as possible. These themes will be addressed in greater detail during the course of this chapter.

The construction experiment

There follows an account of an experiment that was designed to investigate how journalists apply the constructional and interpretive rules practically.

What this part of the study aimed to show was the structure of the news story as defined by the journalists. The experiment allowed an examination of exactly which segments of information, from the case scenario (see appendix I), the journalists rated as being important and which were not important i.e. an information selection and rejection pattern (interpretive rules). It was a test which enabled the author to assess what information journalists regarded as important and how they rated certain aspects of the scenario. It further revealed how important the scientific or environmental information was rated by journalists.

The press release was divided into eight thematic variables and eight source scientific variables. These tables of keyword variables are listed below. These results have also been arranged in a final grid so that the construction patterns can be viewed more clearly (see pages 134 and 138).

Table 3 (a) Thematic Variables Derived from Scenario

V1	Pesticides
V2	Cancer
V3	Water
V4	Illness (Human)
V5	Illness (Wildlife)
V6	Forestry Commission
V7	Benazalox
V8	North East

Table 3 (b) Source Variables Derived from Scenario

V9	Police
V10	Quotes (Non-specialists)
V11	Quotes (Specialists)
V12	Scientists
V13	Doctors
V14	Media
V15	Sources
V16	Named Victims

Table 4 Groupings of Scientific Variables

V1 Chemical Pesticides
    Chemical Poisoning
	V4 Benazalox
	     Phenoxyalkanoic
	     Biological Magnification

V2 Insecticides
     DDT, Lindane
     Organics
     Organophosphates
     Organochlorines
     Herbicides
     Pest Control
	V5 Inhalation
	     Absorption
	     Ingestion

V3 Carcinogenic
     Mutagenic, genetic
	V6 Neurotoxicity
	     Toxic
	     Cancer
	     Respiratory Effects

Table 5 Results of Construction Exercise (general variables)

Percentages	V1	V2	V3	V4	V5	V6	V7	V8	V9	V10	V11	V12	V13	V14	V15	V16
1-10	XXX X	X		XXXX X	XXX X					X	XX			XX		
11-20	X XX X		X	XX X	XX X	XXX	X					X		X		
21-30	XX	X		X	X			X		X	X	XX X	XXX	X	X 0	X X
31-40		X	X 0 X X	X	XX			X		X				X		XX X
41-50	X X			X	X X	XX		X	0		X X			XX		XX X
51-60	XX X		XX		X	X	X	X			X	XX XX				X 0 X
61-70	0		XX X	X		X				X	XX X	X		XX		X X
71-80	XXX X			X		X		X		X	XX X XX			XX		XX X X
81-90	X										XX X			X		X
91-100	X							X			X			X		X

Eight reporters took part in the construction exercise. Each journalist was assigned a position within the variable/percentage box (see below). The crosses show where the journalists referred to the corresponding variable and also where in the article this reference occurred. The circles represent a greater density of variables i.e. where a respondent has used the variable more than once.

Table 6 The Distribution of Journalists within Grid

P1	P2	P3
P4	B1	B2
B3	B4	

The journalists who took part in this exercise were kept anonymous but the table above shows where, within the square, the press reporters and the broadcast reporters were situated.

Discussion

It is evident from the grid that there are certain areas of coverage which are regarded as important by the majority of respondents. Taking into account that 1-20% is regarded as the beginning of the story, 21-70% is the middle and 71-100% is the end of the story, it can be seen that the heaviest concentration of data appears within the 1-20% section, at variables 1, 4 and 5. However variables 11, 14 and 16 show definite patterns in the lower-middle and end of story sections (61-100%).

Overall variables 1, 4 and 5 which are the terms "pesticides", "human illness" and "animal illness" display the highest concentration of data. This is to be expected as this is the information that is the most important in news value terms. The term "pesticides" is the only variable that has been referred to consistently throughout the story. It is, therefore, perceived to be the most common term that is recognised by all sections of the audience/readership.

The results confirm that the human interest news value is the most important information in the story. This is the line or "lead" (Tiffen, 1989, p64) that draws the reader or the viewer into the story. It is, in effect, the point of audience interaction with the text. This has been revealed by the fact that variables 4 and 5 are heavily used at the beginning of the journalists' stories (1-20%). Apparently, of secondary relevance is the geographic positioning of the incident. Very few journalists referred to the north east indicating that the story was perhaps strong enough to stand by itself without the mention of a north east line.

Other significant trends show that variables 11 and 16 are regarded by journalists as less important in that they have included them further down their stories. Reference to these variables, "scientists" and "quotes (specialist)" (the latter refers to quotations from specialists e.g. scientists and doctors) exist in concentrated blocks on the grid. This also confirms the journalists' accounts of news practice because they stated that the importance of scientific information is secondary to the facts of the incident. This is substantiated by the more detailed study of the selection and rejection of scientific information outlined below.

Variable 14 gives a good account of the other sources which journalists might approach for the story e.g. the Scottish Office, the Water Purification Board...(operational factors). But the indication from the grid suggests that these other references would be resigned to a lower part of the story indicating their lack of importance. Some journalists stated that these would be used to pad out a story so that it fitted the correct size of news hole.

> ...A good front page lead is 40cms...how long it is to fit the page. You have to have....25 paragraphs of information to fit the news story. You can start off with just one fact that you know and you can pad the rest out with suppositions and quotes and reported speech and hearsay. If that one line is good enough, you can pad out a story to 40cms. It's not the case that something doesn't get reported because you don't have enough information about it. It depends on how important you think it is. [LNJ]

The journalist, above, reinforces how the categories work together. He states that the lack of information (an operational function) has no bearing on construction, it depends on how newsworthy it is (an evaluative function). This underlines the intertextuality of the different rule categories and proves that they are used in combinations by journalists.

The remaining variables have been referred to very infrequently by the journalists. The second variable, "cancer", is not, generally, used by the journalists as many of them maintained that to refer to this term at such an early stage of the coverage would be a negation of their social and professional responsibilities. It would cause unnecessary concern among the audience or readership at a time when the tests carried out by scientists were not conclusive. Variables 7 and 13 have been used very little and it can be concluded that the respondents rated these as being of negligible importance. The ninth variable "Benazalox" is discussed more fully below. The grid shows that variable 15 "named victims" has also been used infrequently but whether this is because the people involved would not normally be named at this stage in the coverage, or whether the respondents found it difficult to invent a realistic story is not clear. It may have been that the journalists were constrained by the differing news values. Consequently, these news stories may have been shorter than the ones which did contain an Aberdeen line, and when the facts were prioritised the victims' names were, therefore, viewed as irrelevant.

There are no significant differences between the ways in which environment correspondents and non-specialist reporters construct the news story. The rules are apparently standard construction procedures for all journalists.

[You cover this] from a journalist's view first because it is not a piece you are researching or a background piece or an analysis, so you have to treat it as a news story. You need to sort out the news story initially and you would do that strictly from a journalistic point of view. Then I can think about the deeper environmental questions to ask. [EC2(n)]

Similarly, there are no definite trends which suggest that the press and broadcast journalists write their news stories in different ways. Although it may be suggested that broadcast reporters sometimes, due to the pragmatics of the news process, cover the news in a superficial way, there is really no evidence from the construction exercise to underline this.

Contrary to the literature and the journalists who took part in the experiment, there is little difference between the broadcast and print journalists. The ways in which the journalists selected and discarded the specific scientific variables is discussed below. The groupings of scientific variables can be seen on page 133.

Table 7 Depicting the Respondents' Use of Scientific Variables

Percentages	V1	V2	V3	V4	V5	V6
1-10	X X X X	X	X	X		
11-20	X X X					X
21-30	X	O X X X	X			
31-40		O	O	X		X
41-50	X X			X	X	
51-60	X X		X X	X		
61-70	X X	X	X			
71-80	X	O	O X	X		
81-90	X	X	X	X		
91-100		X		X		X

Discussion

Generally, the journalists used very little scientific information in their stories and when they did use it, it tended to be "diluted" or popular science. The terminology they used was populist and their work was free of "jargon". The groupings of terms were again drawn out from the press release and it is evident that very few of them were used in the stories.   It is significant that when the journalists did make use of terms they tended to do so in the final two thirds of this report. Variable 1 (which may be seen as a grouping of the most populist terminology) was used consistently throughout but also noticeably at the beginning of the stories. It is not clear from the grid exactly which keywords journalists chose from the groups, therefore, it must be stated that from Variable 2 "Organics"

138

was the term referred to. Again from Variable 2, "herbicides" was relied on heavily and "organics" was the term referred to. "Herbicides" was relied on heavily and "genetic", "mutagenic" and "carcinogenic" very infrequently. "Benazalox" was the only term used in Variable 4 and none of the journalists referred to any within grouping 5. Finally the terms "cancer" and "toxic" were the only two used in Variable 6. It can be concluded therefore that it is the simple, populist terms which have been referred to the most frequently. This, however, reinforces what journalists have said about only using the science that they themselves can understand on the lowest level. This function where the journalist acts as an intellectual filter for the audience is discussed more fully later on.

There are again no definite trends which suggest that there are significant differences between how environment correspondents and non-specialist reporters select or reject scientific information. From the discourse sessions all the journalists agreed that very little science would be used in the construction due to both the pragmatics of the process and also the audience's ability to understand very little complex scientific material.

The experiment suggests strongly that journalists do write with the audience in mind. It is, however, apparent that some of them are unaware of this and that the image of the audience is tacit.

The pragmatics of construction

> ...The news story is - or should be - a product of his [journalist's] disciplined perception and his evaluation of the environment, of the social arena from which the story and its characters come and of the bureaucratic climate in which it is written. (Geiber in White (1964), p173)

Former practitioners like Willis (1991) and Harris (1989) talk about the ways in which journalism students are taught to report in logical sequences and that if these are followed directly a natural picture of reality is obtained. This research has revealed that these sequences become routinised by reporters through experience on the job. Willis (1991) stresses though that,

> ...this world of shadows is, for the most part, an unintentionally incomplete or distorted view of reality and if they could, journalists would make it conform even more closely to reality. (Willis, 1991, p11)

Historically, academics have accused journalists of manufacturing the news within particular contexts (Hall, 1972; Gans, 1980) and of mediating an artificial construction as reality. Willis (1991) and others (Harris, 1987; Hodgson, 1989) have started to retaliate by demonstrating that this is not intentional but a symptom of the news process. This is a view echoed by the journalists who were interviewed.

Many of the rules which emerged from discussions with journalists referred to the practical ways in which a news story is constructed, for example, the length of the story, the type of language used and the editing techniques involved. The journalists explained the use of quotes, their preferred writing styles and how they are constrained by the amount of space available from their media.

> A quote brings a story to life. It makes it more...it gives it a human edge because there is someone actually speaking...A story is like an upside down triangle. You start with all the important stuff up near the top, and it kind of tapers down so that when you get to the bottom, it's superfluous information. There are two reasons for that...people don't read every paragraph of every story...they just "taste test" and then they go on to the next one. So it is important to have something that grabs the attention in the first paragraph - the most important information. The other reason is (it's a practical reason for the sub-editor) if the story is too long and has to be cut down. The best way to do that is to chop off the last three paragraphs and if you have the least important at the end, it's not so difficult. [LNJ]

The broadcast and the press journalists differ quite considerably in the ways they construct the news. Television reporters place much more emphasis on the visual components of a story and the press a greater onus on in-depth analysis, photographs and graphics. Time and space are also constraints which serve to underline the apparent superficiality of broadcast news. It is this, in addition to the close attention paid to visual parameters, which has given media critics the opportunity to accuse television news practitioners of disproportionately representing reality. The broadcast journalists replied to this, as follows:

> this one [case 5] is different and highlights things which I haven't explained very much with the others but which is really the first consideration for a television journalist to varying degrees but more so in a news story, that is the pictures. I would ensure that very early on there

was an outside broadcast unit there so that they could squirt pictures all around Britain and around the world. [NBJ1]

...We have been accused of skimming the surface and yes, I'm afraid we do skim the surface because of the nature of television news and there is nothing we can do about it. It means that to truly develop that story [case 1] you are talking about five minutes. Now if I develop that to five minutes you're talking about only having five items a night. I think that to cover an area the size of the one we cover then you need a [lot] more than five items a night. Very often we don't have time to spend on its construction because we're trying to be up to date and as newsy as possible. If a story breaks and comes to our attention within the half an hour to go to transmission, then we only have half an hour to assemble the story. But in an ideal world, which it isn't always, yes if it was a big story we would try and devote a lot of time to it. Time in preparation and time in transmission as well. [LTJ]

The press is also limited by the space made available to them and this is reflected in the writing of articles. The amount of space is conditional upon the number of news stories that are likely to be included on the day.

There is also a question of compression - you're working within the parameters of space in a newspaper. I've always found that this gets forgotton about when the media is being criticised by linguists. There are a number of physical constraints in terms of space in a newspaper. [LNA2]

...The front page of a tabloid...will have one paragraph of reporting and the rest will be just a big block headline and perhaps a head and shoulders photograph of somebody. Broadsheet papers...will arrange the top four or five important stories on their front page. Sometimes you've got a good strong story which you can't make 40cms e.g. if something's the subject of legal proceedings then you are limited in what you can say because of prejudicing a future trial. In many cases you are limited in what you can say. [LNJ]

It is, therefore, not always space and time that can prevent information being disseminated. The journalist is bound by legal constraints as well. This suggests that there are a number of factors inherent in the news process that can prevent the flow of certain kinds of information from source to audience.

It has been noted previously that there are not any specific

141

differences between environment correspondents and non-specialist reporters. This category is no exception. What is noticeable from the specialists' data is that they possess a clearer definition of the audience, and a greater depth of knowledge of the subject area.

> Television is shorter but sometimes you can make more impact...Generally, people closely involved with the story are happier with my radio coverage and that tends to go for the scientists, health experts, doctors etc. This is because I haven't been tied to writing to pictures. Pressure groups vary in their response. They are visually more pleased to get it on television because it makes more impact and they are campaigning groups who want the publicity. [EC(b)]

This is a view echoed by Friedman (1987) when she talks about how pressure groups bombard the media with press releases in exchange for publicity.

Dramatic emphasis

In Jostein Gripsrud's (in Dahlgren and Sparks, 1992) discussion of the aesthetics and politics of melodrama and its application to tabloid news, he states that,

> ...the melodramatic is...an expressionist aesthetic, striving to externalise what is underneath the chaotic and uncertain surface of modern existence. (Gripsrud in Dahlgren and Sparks, 1992, p87)

He suggests that melodrama is a technique used by the popular press to teach the audience life lessons by demonstrating moral forces at work in society e.g. the contest between good and evil. It is argued that this journalistic technique extends not only to the tabloid press but also to the quality broadsheets. There is evidence of this type of construction/interpretive technique in the newspaper text examined at the time of the Braer (Campbell, 1996). The melodrama inextricably linked with the news text on the Braer is no different to any other emotive newsworthy disaster. This value system is exemplified by trends emerging from the news text e.g. subject specialists vs damage to the environment; locals vs Braer crew and captain; environment vs the oil. Gripsrud notes how the use of photography and titles is,

142

...reminiscent of the standardised iconography of emotions found in the melodramatic tradition in theatre, film and television...The popular press...never tires of informing us by way of such melodramatic, redundant, formulaic texts that emotions are underneath the world's seemingly chaotic surface, that politicians and other important people have emotions, too. (Gripsrud in Dahlgren and Sparks, 1992, p88)

The journalists, themselves, revealed that the use of drama as a technique is implicit in the constructional and interpretive rules they practice. However, only some of them acknowledged that there are "legitimate" and "illegitimate" uses of drama. One journalist suggests that the legitimate use is, for example, to issue warnings to the public to create an awareness of the danger of a situation.

This use of the dramatic technique has its source in the journalistic role of social responsibility (see chapter 4). It has already been established that in the editorial setting, it is acceptable for the journalist to overemphasise rather than underplay the event (e.g. the Braer). This phenomenon is explained by the journalist thus,

...in a case [1] like this it's quite easy to [dramatise]...you saw it with the flesh eating virus and everyone just jumped on the bandwagon purely because of the visual image of parts of the body being eaten away. I think it is a contextual problem...very often the media are guilty of [not setting it in context] and there's a sort of drama aspect to it. For certain sectors of the media this is acceptable [providing] they do put it into context. [LNA1]

The aesthetics of drama

Sood [et al] (1987) report that disasters are like drama which contain the relevant inherent qualities common to melodrama. Not least is the capability for capturing public attention and attracting the largest audiences and readerships. It may be argued that in keeping with the "drama" analogy, disaster reports assume unreal qualities that succeed in reversing the audience's suspension of disbelief.

When journalists are challenged about the negativity of the drama rule, they blame the audience saying that they are responding to the needs of this audience or readership. As the one journalist stated, the media have been guilty, in the past, of not putting an event into context i.e.

juxtapositioning the event beside other similar or related events which have been resolved positively or framing the event in correct proportion to other relevant factors. It is when this context is lost that the alignment in the construction process is altered i.e. meanings on the information are changed (see Chapter 2) and only a partial view of reality is obtained.

> Melodrama continues to present its audiences with a "sense-making system", a system which insists that politics or history are only interesting in so far as they affect our everyday life and its conditions, our feelings - fears, anxieties, pleasures. (Gripsrud in Dahlgren and Sparks, 1992, p88)

This function or rather dysfunction of melodrama is evident in the ways the Braer was covered by the local and regional press. It serves to underline the fact that both soft and hard news is treated to a dramatic emphasis in disaster situations.

Melodrama is a technique which particularly enhances the human interest angle on a news story. The journalists, through their discussion of case 2, revealed that the strong human interest angle would make a dramatic line for the story i.e. the fact that the eight year old girl has died. This lead would generate a great deal of coverage.

> That would be one big story with a lot of follow ups...The wee girl would come in for a lot of coverage of her death. We might talk about what she would have done, what she might have done if she'd grown up. It's one of the things which people would read. [ENJ]

Therefore, the use of dramatisation i.e. building up a picture of what the girl's life would have been like had she lived is designed to draw the reader into the story. It is a point of audience interaction. The rationale behind this technique is that the reader identifies vicariously with the victim of the situation thereby becoming emotionally involved with the story.

As the journalists recounted the synthesis of their tasks and described the routines involved in their work, it reinforced the constructed nature of the business. One of the tasks which was identified for case 2 (see appendix I) was the need to locate another child with asthma and draw a contrast between this child and the one who had died. The purposes of this exercise were to illustrate how fortunate the parents of the second child were in still having her/him and also to underline the severity of the environmental problem.

You would try and track down another child who's still alive, with asthma and her parents and get them to say, "we fear the same could happen to our daughter or son". [ENJ]

The use of this type of technique serves to underline the fact that these procedures could influence the construction of the final product. However, journalists talk about their primary aim as being objectivity or impartiality. In journalistic terms this is the highest goal to achieve and is synonymously and inextricably inter-linked with professional credibility. But how is the story balanced? Is the story ever balanced?

The journalists who were interviewed seemed unaware of biasing the news themselves. When questioned further about this area, they indicated that the nature of the news process itself plays an integral part in biasing the end product. Further, the reporters found it very difficult to rationalise how they balance a story because of the tacit nature of this construction rule. The following comment is taken from the discussion of case 3,

...you try and get both sides. Here the two sides to the argument are, the increase in tourism and the damage to the thing which attracts tourists as well. We wouldn't have to support one particular faction. Often the opponents are the strongest...but that's not necessarily taking their side. You often say, "...fierce opposition has been expressed toward or proposed...". You know, you would do it in a balanced way. I would not balance it up by giving three inches to them and three inches to them. It just depends on how it comes along. And that would be about it. [NNJ]

The pragmatics of the construction process influence the rules journalists use and consequently shape the news product. Although, journalists have been criticised for covering environmental or political issues superficially and, therefore, inaccurately (due to the information reduction and altering of meaning), it must be stated that much of this can be attributed to the practicalities of the news process.

In interpreting complex information for the audience or readership the journalist must simplify or dilute the material. This is partly due to the practical reasons above and partly to aid the comprehension of the news consumer. The next sections deal with the problems encountered by reporters in the communication of science or the environment and interpretation patterns that they adopt in order to solve these problems.

The communication of science and the environment

All the journalists agreed that there are difficulties attached to the communication of science, in terms of the complexity of the information and the jargon in which it is codified. In talking about these problems, it was evident that the journalists possess ready-made assumptions about the audience or readership. They assume, for example, that the receivers of the information (audience/readership) cannot make sense of the scientific terminology, nor can they cope with complex concepts. This is perhaps justified in that primary (i.e. information which exists in bibliographies and directories) and even secondary (i.e. the information which is interpreted by scientists) levels of environmental information (see chapter 2) are pluralistic, multidisciplinary and technical.

Historically, scientists have believed that the media misrepresent environmental concepts and theories (Funkhouser, 1973). Conversely, the journalists feel that they have a responsibility to their readers, viewers or listeners to explain as fully as possible the science that is involved in issues. However, as the individual media are bound by the constraints of time and space they (specialists and non-specialists alike) believe it is preferable to include as little science as is necessary.

> The problem with the environment particularly with scientists and researchers is...they rarely appreciate the value of giving their work a public aim. Most of the research is locked up in jargon or in their own head...it is presented in such scientific jargon that it's unreportable and you need a degree to understand it. They don't appreciate the value of their work as news. [LNA2]

The evidence gathered from subject specialists (scientists) (see chapter 3) and journalists reveals a communication stalemate in which both groups of personnel often reinforce their own distorted perceptions of what the other group needs. Specialists, characteristically, view the media as a powerful vehicle through which to describe, explain and publicise their research. However, their main grievances seem to be that issues become oversimplified, reduced to basic black and white terms or that complex theoretical information is diluted and reduced to such an extent that it is meaningless. They have, on occasions, accused the media of distorting their theories and of misinforming the public about scientific and environmental issues.

The news media argue that specialists fail to understand the rapid continuity of the news process, the pressures of deadlines and the immediacy with which the news has to be constructed and disseminated. Scientists, they maintain are apparently unaware of not only the value of their work in news terms, but the necessity to explain clearly in simple terminology the essence of their research for the audience. One of the journalists talked about the complexities of science and the difficulties that occur when attempting to communicate it to a lay audience,

> ...a lot of it is very complex. Global warming is hugely complicated and by simplifying it you can make it meaningless or just inaccurate. By condensing it, it can lose its meanings. I do things on the problems of global warming and I find that my colleagues here, say, "what problems?" The really big environment problems - the ozone layer, global warming, fuel pollution - the scientists, themselves, don't really understand them, so what hope does the environment correspondent have? You just have to say that this has happened and this is what they are all saying. It's really hard. You can make yourself very unpopular because if I go around constantly telling people that global warming is a bad thing they think I'm mad. [EC(b)]

Scientists perceive themselves as victims of the media. The media retaliate, emphasising that the nature of the news process is such that technical information has to be reinterpreted for mediation to the news consumer. The distortion which may occur is not intentional. Burkhart (1992) states,

> ....media messages add to their credibility with audiences: [they] want to convey information accurately and completely. However, dealing with the mass media entails "costs" for environmental professionals: (1) precision will be lost; (2) frustration may result from confronting such media constraints as deadlines or simplification of complex material; (3) control over the message, guaranteed in scientific and professional communication will be lost. (p80)

The perceptual differences between both groups of personnel is accentuated by their opposing agendas and the misunderstanding of each other's priorities.

The journalists outlined the difficulties of the scientific communication as follows,

147

...it's about rendering complex information meaningful to the individual and basically it's a process of waiting until you comprehend what is going on and then a feeling that you're probably at the right level. You just have to develop a kind of general understanding of all areas but you don't have that specialist understanding. [LNJ]

Quite often you are dealing with difficult concepts in terms of science and it's being able to simplify it without getting it wrong and still explain it clearly. [EC1(n)]

The reporters underline the tacitness of the process by talking about developing this critical understanding of the appropriate level at which to pitch the information. I have called this procedure *intellectual filtering* and this journalistic role is discussed below.

The construction of news and the journalists' perceptions of the audience

Tiffen (1989) argues that the audience is a major factor that influences how the journalist writes. Drawing on the idea that the journalist writes with an image of the implied audience or reader in mind, many of the journalists stated that they did not imagine one reader or viewer although that was the way they were taught to write. However, the responses on this theme were mixed,

...no...I don't think of them actively but I've got a gut feeling as I think most journalists have for the audience or the readership. I mean if I started preparing reports while I was viewing my audience as a group of *Sun* readers or a group of *Financial Times* readers then that would affect the nature of coverage and the "feel" of the coverage as well as the content of stories but as it is I can honestly say that I never sat down to try and visualise an average viewer because I don't think there is such a thing. Especially for television, we are rather unlike newspapers - newspapers tend to aim at a niche market, we have to appeal across a pretty wide range. So I don't have a view in my mind of the viewer but I have a feel for what I think they might be interested in. [NBJ1]

You always have to imagine the readers. I don't know if I have a reader in my head as such but I always imagine that someone is...when I'm looking at my stuff on the screen, I imagine that I'm someone else and would I be able to understand it? Even if it is something which is not necessarily scientific but it's something I know about as it's something I've covered for 3 months or whatever. It's just become common knowledge in my mind. It might not be common knowledge in someone else's mind. I always step back and say (a) is it interesting and (b) can I understand it. You don't really take into account different types of readership, every reader is much the same. But yes you do have an image of the readership. If you don't then you end up writing needless nonsensical stuff. [LNA1]

Work carried out by DePool and Shulman (reported in White, 1964) into the ways in which journalists construct the news product, shows that reporters are influenced by images of the intended audience. They talk about the "picures in [journalists'] heads" which appear to be congruent with the images of the audience/readership and which are created by editorial and organisational factors.

They're quite an informed audience...If I had an image of who would be interested in my stories, it would be just the person in the street...but behind that there is another image which is the university professor who will almost certainly write me a letter saying that I've misunderstood or there is a bit more research that I should have looked into and they're very much the vocal part of the audience. [EC(b)]

This journalist imagines a range of characters and so does not limit him/herself to a stereotypical view of the audience. This, in turn, has an influence on how he/she writes and constructs the product. This person, being a bi-media correspondent i.e. radio and television, goes on to acknowledge a slight difference between her/his perceptions of the two audiences.

I have perhaps in my head a slight sense of difference in the ways a radio audience pays attention...it's probably the same people...but it's...you perhaps expect people listening to radio to listen more closely to what you are saying than someone watching television. [EC(b)]

[I don't have a picture of the readership in my head]...with any newspaper readership...you very quickly develop a feel for the style. Every newspaper has a style. It's not something you learn. It's something you are aware of when you've worked at the paper for a certain amount of time. You learn to have an idea of who will read a scientific story in the Scotsman which will be very different from a scientific story in the tabloids. [EC2(n)]

The origins of these images are unclear and the journalists found it difficult to articulate exactly where they came from. Most journalists stated that they paid particular attention to the market research carried out by the organisation and also the feedback that they receive directly from the "news consumers". These images are reinforced over time (as are the other rules) and become tacit through their continued repetition.

Through these constructional and interpretive rules, journalists make and sustain assumptions about their respective audiences, for example, that viewers/readers can only understand diluted versions of scientific concepts or populist terminology. The local news agency journalists explained how on occasions, they prepare two different versions for both the tabloids and the "quality" broadsheets,

> ...for the tabloids, it's a fairly simple case of "humans been taken ill because of such and such" and fairly straightforward. You'd need a few quotes from people to back it all up and that would be it. A tabloid would probably make an average of about 14 or 15 paragraphs, and that would be the lead story on a given page. For a broadsheet like *The Scotsman* or *The Telegraph* then you could perhaps triple the size of the story and be as scientific as you like. You'd still cover the basic story but write it in bigger words...to be quite blunt about the whole thing and you can have enough scientific stuff as long as you understand it. [LNA2]

This journalist has given voice to the classic stereotypical assumption of which journalists are aware and on which they base this practice, that tabloid readers are less intelligent than broadsheet readers. In their defence, several of the reporters registered their disapproval of this taken-for-granted assumption but acknowledged that it is a stereotype that is embedded in newspaper culture and is irreversable at present.

The journalist, above, also underlines the fundamental differences between the construction process for tabloids and broadsheets and reinforces the alternative types of information which each demands. A study carried out by Funkhouser in 1969 demonstrated that the higher the proportion of university graduates in the readership, the more complex the language in the news reports (Funkhouser, 1969). The journalists indicated that this may be so as regards journalistic semantics but that complex scientific theories will still require to be explained with the lowest common level of comprehension. Therefore, regardless of broadcast or tabloid status, complicated environmental information has to be explained in the most simplistic terms.

DePool and Shulman's Reference Group Phenomenon or Theory stated that images of the intended audience/readership "enters the author's flow of associations at the same time of composition and influences what he writes or says" (DePool and Shulman in White, 1964). The key findings from DePool and Shulman's experiment showed that the construction process provided the journalist with psychological gratification that contributed to a fantasy state. In this readers would admire and praise them and the reporter achieved a worthy status that enabled him to affect the social and cultural processes (DePool and Shulman in White, 1964).

> The news writing situation...is an instance of one-way communication to a secondary audience. The gratification arising from such activities are largely deference and power, either real or fantasized. The communicator is the teacher, instructor, guide i.e. the authority figure over the passive audience. (DePool and Shulman in White, p156)

The audience is not passive and the journalists, whilst accepting the power of the media, showed that, in general, reporters perceive their role as one of social responsibility, maintaining both self-set and professional journalistic standards. This is discussed later in greater detail. One of the journalists summarised his professional role as follows,

> ...the most important journalistic technique is to explain and translate it into simple terms i.e. stories on any subject. A good journalist should be able to write about a political event, about an industrial story or an environmental disaster...about a whole range of things by distilling the information...by gathering the information and then distilling it into a simple, accessible format. It's got to be accessible...so I'd put in just enough science to be able to explain a story. You have to re-read it because you have to be sure that it is understandable. [EC2(n)]

This journalist underlines the need for simplicity in the distilling of scientific information, and in doing so emphasises again that the perception of the intended audience is indeed the rationale for the journalist's role as an intellectual filter within the construction process.

Most journalists write with an image of the audience or readership in mind and this is one of the factors which influences how they construct the news. It is also evident that journalists think about what they write but not about how they write. This process has been referred to as instinctive by several of the journalists who maintained that they do not think about

151

the writing process as such.

The journalist as an intellectual filter

The secondary stage of the model (chapter 2) describes the construction part of the news process, by defining the way journalists interpret information for the audience, as a filter action.

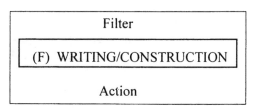

Figure 15 Excerpt from Secondary Stage of Model

This means that journalists having identified the story (evaluative) and gathered the information (operational), are then required to absorb and assess the information so that they can decide what to include or ignore. They can, finally, estimate how to construct the story in order to best explain the complexity of issues for the audience or readership.

It is evident that there are several rules inherent in the interpretive process. These are that the journalist simplifies an issue for the audience and that the journalist waits until he or she comprehends the issue and reaches the appropriate level to begin communicating it to the reader. This last rule seems to be a subconscious process as there are no yardsticks against which to evaluate this levelling. As a result of these rules, assumptions are made by journalists about what the audience wants and what they can cope with. This levelling of information to suit the audience or readership involves reducing or expanding concepts depending on the issue.

> [The environment] has suffered because it has been [regarded as] popular science and to make it understandable we have had to put pretty pictures on it and tell it in very simple terms. That has made it quite simplistic in itself when actually deep down it hasn't been. It's like the pictures I saw today of the Hubble Spacecraft - it's literally....child's picture book stuff -

"Here is Mars - doesn't it look amazing? Here is its star - doesn't it look amazing?" He [science correspondent] knows the science and he will have been told why the pictures are important and what they now show but by the time they translate that into television it is simplified. [EC(b)]

This journalist implies that the medium affects the message and that the information is simplified for the benefit of the audience and by the pragmatics of construction. A key difference (already examined) between the specialist and non-specialist correspondents is the depth of knowledge that the specialists possess about the subject areas. Although the science and environment journalists have only a fraction of the expertise that research scientists have, they are aware of the main theories and issues in their fields. They are, however, limited in the amount of scientific information they can include, by the constraints of their media and the perceptions of the audience. Some of the journalists who were not specialist correspondents stated that in the event of an environmental "disaster" they would consult environment journalists who could explain the issues to them. This is yet another level through which the information passes and with each stage the possibility of distortion becomes more likely.

...You would have specialist writers who would be able to...who would know how to speak to the scientists on level terms - an environmental correspondent, for example, and you would probably ask them to speak to the scientists to put some of the scientific jargon, that you've got on your data sheet, into layman's terms. [ENJ]

It has been established that all journalists (press and broadcast; specialists and non-specialists) cover environmental issues as straight news stories. Further, reporters, regardless of their position in the editorial chain or their specialisms, include very discrete amounts of science in their news constructions. The journalists talked about the economy of language, implying that, on a practical level, the constraints of space and time preclude the necessity for complex scientific information in news. The journalists talked about levelling,

I don't mind the science but it has to be in layman's terms because I can't do a story on the presumption that I have got 30000 scientists listening. I've got 30000 punters whose average news diet would be the Press and Journal or the Record so we have to go at that level. We can't go at the level of the New Scientist or the BMJ. We have to simplify it down or

153

have them simplify it down for us. [LRJ]

The majority of the journalists stated that they would get the experts to break down the science into its constituent parts and explain the theories or they would attempt to decode the science themselves and check with the expert before using the information.

> The science would be kept to an absolute minimum...The only thing that you might want to say is that you might want to mention the name of the product that is causing the illnesses, and more importantly what it does to people - makes you sick or gives you headaches etc. Little of this in the press release would be used in an article - very very little...you'd be more likely to get some press friendly expert to translate it into layman's terms rather than jargonese. [ENJ]

> I can go to a scientist and say "can you please make that as simplified as you can? What does this mean?"... "...well, it means that there has been a concentration of it or whatever in the soil there and it is not draining away. It is built up and now with the heavy rainfall it has been washed away and has ended up in the stream."... If I don't know what it means, hopefully I can find someone who can tell me what it means and they can explain to my listeners what it means. That's always what I would aim to do - keep it as simple as possible. [LRJ]

Several of the journalists mentioned the fact that they gauged the right level at which to pitch the information for the audience by assessing their own comprehension of issues.

> My approach would be to find out about the science...to attempt to understand it myself. When I come to write it up I find time and time again that ... there isn't space for it by the time you explain the basic story there is very little space to put in much science and even if I do put in some it won't hit you as being science with a capital "S", it'll be my understanding of science. If I have time I'll go back to the scientist and say, "look, if I put it like this so that a general audience can understand it, will I still be accurate?" If they say yes...then that's how I'll do it...I would try and explain...what it is that has caused the health problems and I'd try to do that in lay terms. [EC(b)]

This is not a foolproof test used by all journalists. One reporter in particular talked about having to block out his own knowledge so as not to bias the construction part of the process and to lower his powers of comprehension in order to correctly estimate that of the reader.

> ...I'd want all this information explained i.e. from the point of view of
> transposing it into readable newscopy. I'd have to be able to understand it
> myself first. As a journalist when you're being trained you are told to use
> the acid test of only reporting what you understand. It's not a question of
> what I understand as a graduate...I've got to lower my processes of
> understanding and take it down to the lowest common denominator i.e. to
> what the average person would understand and sometimes you go over the
> score. [LNJ]

This journalistic test leads inevitably to simplification and it is apparently
preferable to oversimplify rather than undersimplify in order to catch a
higher number of readers.

The following comment demonstrates the form that case 2 would
take and the assumptions made by the journalist about his intended
audience,

> ...you'd have a main simple human interest story. Then, inside, you might
> have a more in-depth analysis on the debate and you probably would only
> bring the science into a simple form - a little panel which is beside the big
> story and there you might have all these fancy names, the various studies
> that have pointed to links, in a very easily accessible format. It has to be
> that way or people would stop reading. If there are two many long words,
> people stop reading. I would myself. It's boring. [ENJ]

The journalists referred, several times, to oversimplification which
they regard as unavoidable and a symptom of the news process. Many
pointed out that their role was to act as a mediator between the scientist
and the lay person and that in order to bridge the considerable gap it is
necessary to explain concepts as clearly as possible and to disregard
scientific terminology. One of the techniques or rules which journalists
use to do this is to write the news by including "signposts" which are
terms or descriptions of similar situations that are familiar to the audience.
Reporters in a sense construct the story from within the context of
previous comparable incidents e.g. the use of the term DDT to illustrate
the effect of the chemical pesticide (see case 1). This rule is essentially
putting the story in a context previously known and accepted by the
audience.

155

I think as soon as you start talking about organophosphates, you turn off most of the people who might otherwise be interested. Lindane and DDT...if you mention DDT then I think that's something that people are already familiar with...so I might mention that kind of brand and mention the fact that there have been problems with it. But beyond that I am unlikely to get into the real science. I see, here that it can be taken by inhalation...I would say that but I wouldn't go beyond that because I don't think people would be particularly interested. [EC(b)]

We might put in herbicide but the actual chemical names...we would probably keep out unless it happened to be a well known brandname. It's a question of identification. We might mention something like DDT. They don't really know what it is but they've heard of it. They've got a rough idea that it is not good. [LNA2]

Tertiary model: a complete statement

If the news process could be described chronologically, the execution of the different sets or categories of rules would be ordered in this manner - evaluative (1) (chapter 6); operational (2) (chapter 7); and constructional/interpretive (3) with the editorial ones (chapter 5) being applied actively throughout.

The previous four chapters have in turn described and analysed different rule categories from within the context of the tertiary stage of the model. The final section of this chapter summarises and concludes the discussion of the model by demonstrating its composite nature and reinforcing how the different types of rules fit together within the news process.

At each stage in the tertiary model the categories are influenced by practical constraints. These are shown by directional arrows on the map. The most common pragmatic factors of the news process, as defined by the journalists in the sample, were space and time. These factors (which are related to editorial rules and, therefore, reinforce how the categories influence each other) tend to demonstrate the differences between the broadcast and print media. Journalists operate within a "stop-watch culture" (Schlesinger, 1977) and this time constraint is at "the centre of decision-making and of news control...usually related to the daily cycle" (Watson and Hill, 1993, p90). Immediacy is generally regarded by academics as a news value but it may also be considered as a pragmatic influence on the construction of news. The nature of news is concerned with immediacy. An event should be reported as close to the incidental time as possible. It is this factor which limits the scope of environmental coverage because the environment tends to exist not so much as singular, isolated events but as collective issues with long term implications. For the environment to exist as news there needs to be a "trigger" incident which is newsworthy enough to allow it precedence over other news items. Watson and Hill (1993) point out that,

> ...the danger with such emphasis on immediacy is that news tends to be all foreground and little background, all events and too little context, all current happening and too little concentration on the historical and cultural background to such events. (Watson and Hill, 1993, p90)

Space is another factor that has editorial and evaluative implications. Editorial decisions are based on the prioritisation of newsworthy items in relation to the amount of space available in the newspaper (discounting material from other departments such as advertising). Similarly, the news is ordered hierarchically in the news schedule and this order is dependent on the news sense of the particular editor in charge. News sense is the tacit knowledge which journalists and editorial personnel acquire after the routinisation of the process.

Newsworthy issues are assessed using news values. According to Watson and Hill (1993) who refer to the work of Cohen and Young (1973), issues will be covered if they fulfil the news value criteria. Events or issues have a better chance at being covered if, they are clear, unexpected, have appeared before, seem larger than they are in reality, and if they are geographically relevant. The journalists emphasised the fact that the most important values were human interest and geographic relevance. They did mention other values briefly but did not rate them as highly. This was due to the design of the methodology that allowed the sample of journalists only to reveal those values which were relevant to the environmental issues they were presented with.

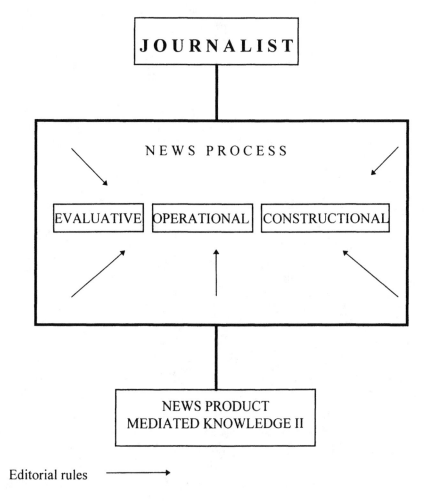

Editorial rules ⟶

Figure 16 Tertiary Stage of Model (simplified)

Collectively, the different rules act as the mechanism by which the news product is constructed and disseminated. This product contributes to the ways in which the audience or readership makes sense of the world around them. This point is marked on the bottom of the tertiary model. Many studies have been carried out to investigate the influence of news on the audience - for example how news language affects the powers of comprehension, (Fowler, 1991; Bell, 1991; Van Dijk, 1990); how news is politically biased (Rachline, 1991; Koch, 1990). This study has not been concerned, primarily, with the receivers of the news product; however, it is necessary to conclude this chapter by turning our attention to the product the audience consumes. If the news is constructed (as Rachline, 1990, suggests) within particular social and political contexts and journalists themselves make assumptions about the world then the news is undeniably a factor which enables people to make sense of things around them. Furthermore, it is a subjective construction which is put together by people who themselves are influenced by their own perceptions of social reality. It is this reality which is constructed through the product,

> ...as the hegemonic ideology reflected in and by the news media represents, re-presents and re-creates the relations of power that characterise the social order, a redefinition of the standards and purpose of the press will not be met without resistance - systemic, institutional and individual. (Rachline, 1990, p134)

Consequently, the tertiary stage adds knowledge to the model in that it highlights and demonstrates in detail the routines or recipe knowledge that is inherent in the news process. It shows the reduction and distillation of information, the journalists' information selection processes and the information sources that are used most frequently. Ultimately, it depicts that each category of rules directs and influences the end product and therefore the newly transformed mediated knowledge of the preliminary stage of the model. It indicates how this finally leads to the journalistic construction of environmental reality.

This chapter has described and analysed the constructional and interpretive rules implicit in the news process. The constructional rules have been identified as those used in the writing, editing and presentation of news. The interpretive rules are concerned with the codification and ultimate simplification of scientific or environmental information for the intended audience. These categories have been discussed at the same time due to the inextricable ways in which they are inter-related. An

159

examination of the information selection and rejection patterns of journalists and implicitly, therefore, the ways they interpret scientific information has been included. Further, an investigation of the various techniques used to write the articles or scripts e.g. dramatic emphasis and the ways in which these are influenced by the pragmatics of the construction process, has been carried out. Themes such as the communication of science and the environment, and the relationship of news values to the writing process emphasising the ways in which each category influences the others, have been developed. In addition, in-depth consideration has been given to the construction and interpretive methods which journalists use through their perceptions of the audience.

Conclusions

This work developed from the idea that as journalists construct and disseminate the product to the audience or readership a particular version or interpretation of social reality is created. This interpretation is subjective because the journalist's perception of an issue is shaped by the organisation's value system. Starting with the idea that environmental information is pluralistic and complex, the following ideas were explored. These were that information changes according to the ways in which it is interpreted and that the flow of environmental information is redirected and influenced by the news process. It was argued that primary or unmediated knowledge is altered into a popularised, commercial form and it appears to have been simplified due to the interpretive journalistic process. The work addressed these claims through the development of a multi-stage model. This model existed in three parts (**preliminary**, **secondary** and **tertiary**). The preliminary stage demonstrated the information flow from unmediated or primary information (KNOWLEDGE I) through levels at which different groups of personnel retrieve and interpret the information, thereby, changing the meanings inherent in it. The last level is the news product or mediated information (KNOWLEDGE II) which is disseminated to the audience or readership. The secondary stage of the model evolved as a result of the application of new data (gathered from journalists in semi-structured interviews) to the preliminary stage. The model was revised, therefore, in light of new evidence from practitioners. The secondary stage described the news process in greater detail and from within a particular reporting context i.e. a hypothetical ecological incident or disaster. It demonstrated the different information sources which journalists consult e.g. the library or scientific specialists. Further, it considered part of the construction process where journalists act as an intellectual filter for the audience (a theme developed extensively in the tertiary stage of the model) or where they simplify complex and technical environmental information for the intended reader or viewer.

Journalists use taken-for-granted procedures or rules when they practice the news process and over a period of time these rules are routinised by the repetition of the same sequence of procedures and ultimately become tacit.

Berger and Luckmann's "The Social Construction of Reality" (1967) argues that knowledge is a social phenomenon which can be described and critically examined. Their work emphasises the importance of language in signifying knowledge and proved to be relevant to the investigation into the knowledge systems that journalists use to mediate environmental news. The book aimed to develop an understanding of the everyday knowledge which journalists utilise to construct the news product. It was designed to explore the idea that when journalists evaluate, interpret and write the news, they mediate a contextual version of social reality which is conditional, in part, upon their particular image of the audience.

Environmental information is pluralistic and complex. The findings from the T.I.D. analysis support the idea that the nature of the information changes due to the process through which journalists interpret and construct the news. There was evidence to suggest (see chapter 8) that information is reduced to manageable segments, the meanings of which are radically simplified for audience consumption. The work has supplied a rationale for this process. Firstly, that this enabled the journalist to satisfy the basic common comprehension level and secondly, the editorial demand to fill a particular size of news hole.

> ...[First] news may be analysed as a "speech act" model, a relativistic conception of news according to which any report of a current event counts as news and is newsworthy by virtue of its being published. On this view the news and the newsworthy are created, not discovered, by the press through its act of publication - they are "whatever the news people say they are". Second, newsworthiness may be analysed in terms of the degree of importance or significance, of the news item in question. Third, it may be analysed in terms of people's interests. (Cohen, 1994, p8)

Cohen above, is reviewing Halberstam's paper "A Prolegomenon For A Theory of News", and makes a valid point in saying that the very nature of the news process is such that news is created by the news media at the very instance it is published. This is not the only way that the news process and therefore, by definition, the news product can be interpreted. News is constructed within a specific editorial and organisational context. This implies that news exists as a number of different representations, each being manifested through diverse value systems. Certain types of

162

environmental issues are more newsworthy than others. One reason for this may be attributed to the fact that certain issues are high on the public and political agendas. This is ironic in that these issues become important in news terms because of the awareness which is generated through the media. Other reasons are that environmental issues generally do not possess hard news qualities unless the story is of "disasterous" proportions e.g. Chernobyl, the Braer. Environmental issues sometimes involve mere assertions and the fact that continuing scientific research is embedded in such issues means that newsworthiness is low.

The evaluative rules were concerned with the ways in which journalists approach environmental issues and assess their newsworthiness. This is done with a knowledge of the organisational policy in mind and this knowledge is tacit. For example, reporters know whether or not an issue is likely to be included in the schedule or newspaper because they apply news values which have been developed by the organisation.

The operational rules consisted of the information gathering strategies involved in the news process. It is this category which underlines how important scientific subject specialists are as sources of information to journalists when covering the environment, thereby substantiating the claims of the preliminary and secondary stages of the model. The book argues that media organisations encourage journalists to rely on human sources for information as opposed to library based literature or electronic information. Evidence, from the journalists themselves, states that the pragmatics of the news process prohibits them from wading through the wealth of scientifically complex information which can be retrieved from impersonal sources. Analysis revealed that there were no great differences between the specialist reporters and the non-specialist reporters in terms of the types of sources they would use. With the specialist reporter working constantly in the environmental field, how reasonable is it to suggest that the journalist has evolved as a subject specialist in his/her own right? This would depend on the definition of subject specialist. A journalist having built up even a credible working knowledge of the subject area is not going to attain the same depth of understanding that an environmental scientist has. Therefore, even possessing a degree or equivalent qualification in environmental science or related discipline, the journalist cannot not be regarded as a subject specialist within the scientific arena. However, taking into account the amount of experience this type of journalist possesses through the continued reinforcement of environmental reporting, it is reasonable to assume the journalist is a specialist within the field of journalism.

The constructional and interpretive rules were discussed together due to the fact that although they were analytically distinct, in practice they are inter-dependent and are applied by journalists at the same time. This category like the operational one, supported the secondary stage of the model (chapter 2). It dealt with the rules which govern the organisation of the raw information, for example, the writing and editing techniques involved in the construction of the product. At the same time, however, it also examined the interpretive rules, for example, the reduction of the scientific information implicit in which is the journalistic function of intellectual filtering.

Finally, the tertiary stage of the model described the routine processes which journalists carry out when constructing the news. It demonstrated the different rule categories and how these interlink or influence each other. Collectively these rules act as the catalyst by which the news is constructed and mediated. The tertiary stage complements and completes the preliminary and secondary stages of the model, which described the interaction between journalists and sources, the procedures and strategies used by reporters to construct the news via the news process and the information flow which occurs from source to product. It provided detailed micro-analysis of the news process which promotes understanding of the methods used to transform KNOWLEDGE I from an unmediated state into the mediated news product.

The research involved an analysis of the methods which news personnel use to interpret, mediate and package information into an intelligible format for the audience. Particular attention was also paid to the manner in which information is constructed into a popularised format for social consumption. Overall, the work has examined the rules journalists used to evaluate the newsworthiness of environmental issues, the sources which are consulted for information e.g. libraries and subject specialists and those used to write the stories.

In conclusion, journalists construct the news product through a process of "taken-for-granted" rules or procedures. Therefore, this book is not only an extensive investigation into the human behavioural elements of news making in Scotland but also a detailed examination of the information processes implicit within news construction. The focus has centred on the use of environmental information because of its multi-disciplinary, complex, scientific nature but the research has widespread, more general applicability, for example, there are other subject areas to which the work could be applied such as business, politics or law.

There is scope for future research in a reception analysis study to assess not only the effect of news on the audience or readership but also to determine the extent to which the social community constructs environmental reality based on news information. This work only considers the audience from within the context of the journalist's perception of his/her intended readership or audience as he/she constructs the product. Therefore, there is potential for a study of this nature which might make use of a qualitative ethnographic methodology and could focus on Scotland.

The notion of contextualisation (chapter 6) or the ways in which journalists use previous reporting experience to facilitate the coverage of particular issues, is an interesting area which could also be developed. Further, there is scope for research into the mental or cognitive mappings used by journalists to reinforce information strategies. Extensions of this work might make use of more quantitative approaches, e.g. cognitive psychological methodologies.

Much research, particularly in the United States, lends itself to the study of the news process within specific contexts such as objectivity, or the dissemination and effect of the news on the audience. Previous investigation has been carried out into the news gathering or information strategies of journalists. This book has stressed the importance of both these facets of the process and emphasised the necessity to study these together with the constructional and interpretive procedures. It is argued that without studying the news process holistically no critical understanding of the integrationalist function of these different rules can be achieved.

This work has attempted to contribute to a deeper understanding of the human processes associated with news making. The identification and elicitation of the rules implicit in the news process will enable us to understand better the future development of journalism.

The purpose of the book has been to explain and critically evaluate the process by which journalists construct, interpret and mediate environmental news. It has contributed to the provision of an important awareness and detailed understanding of the ways in which the media represent and communicate environmental reality in Scotland.

Our perceptions of the natural world are, of course, both real and illusory. The certainty of what is reality and what is illusion...is knowable only from points of reference that we accept as defining these two states. These references are not built into the germ-line cells as part of our genetic constitutions: they are developed by culture and by experience and retained within our memory. (Morris, 1986, p14)

It is for reasons such as these, that practitioners and academics alike may be interested in this study. The work will, hopefully, facilitate journalists to become aware of the job they have routinised and more importantly of the synthesis of the rules which they "take-for-granted". It is hoped that this book will allow practitioners to understand the news process objectively, enabling them to distance themselves from the inevitably subjective view of the profession that they possess.

Appendix I Case Scenarios

Case 1: The Use of Chemical Pesticides in Agriculture

The use of artificial, chemical pesticides in agriculture and other food related industries has concerned scientists since their initiation.

The main classes of chemical pesticides are herbicides (to kill weeds); fungicides (to control [pathogenic fungi); nematocides (to eradicate the eelworm); and insecticides (to kill insects).

Insecticides can be further divided into two groups, organophosphates and organochlorines. Many of the organophosphates are extremely poisonous and attack pests through the nervous system. In many cases they are unstable i.e. they can be broken down by the environment. Parathion and TEPP are two of the most unstable, poisonous organophosphates.

Organochlorines are stable ie non-biodegradable and have caused extensive environmental pollution. These compounds are very soluble in lipids or fat. Their biochemical action could cause changes in fertility and enzyme action. These organic or synthesized chemicals e.g. DDT (Dichlorodiphenyltrichloroethane), Lindane, Dieldrin (all now banned) can be spread as wind blown dust.

Herbicides are the most widely used form of pest control in the UK today. They are a group of organic chemicals, used to destroy or control the growth of weeds. These can be subdivided into three groups - selective (destruction of certain plants e.g. Benazalox), residual (applied at seed time) or translocated (sprayed onto leaves).

There has been concern about the possible effects of herbicides on humans as some are highly toxic, and may have carcinogenic or mutagenic effects.

Benazalox is a crop herbicide, containing benzolin, a compound derived from benzoic acid. It is a member of the phenoxyalkanoic acid group. This chemical is commonly used in the north east of Scotland, in the production of oil seed rape. It should not be sprayed if raining or windy. It is extremely irritating to the skin and eyes.

Toxic substances enter the food chain by a process known as Biological Magnification. During this, the toxins become more concentrated at each higher stage in the food chain. Top level carnivores (this can be humans) are most badly affected as the poisons are condensed as each level ingests the one below. For example the compound DDT which is soluble in lipids or fat tissues, collects there and is magnified at each level in the chain.

The effects of chemical pesticides depend on a number of criteria, e.g. dosage, type of exposure, the general health of the person and how easily the chemical can be absorbed. Pesticides are generally taken in by inhalation, through the mucus membranes eg eyes, nose; through the skin; or by ingestion. The body's metabolism can make the pesticide more water-soluble which can be excreted but it can also increase the toxic effect. Similarly, when the simultaneous use of two or more different chemical pesticides takes place, the resulting interaction can create a substance which is either more or less toxic. Those which may be more toxic can also be mutagenic or carcinogenic. The organochlorines cause chloracne and lesions of the central nervous system and organophosphates eg organophosphorous induces behavioural changes and delayed neurotoxicity. The chronic effects of hazardous chemical pesticides include bone marrow effects e.g. aplastic anaemia; cancer (in particular, respiratory cancer amongst humans working with arsenical pesticides); male infertility and neurotoxicity. These are more often linked with occupational situations. Non-occupational exposure examples include, accidental poisoning by ingesting food which was contaminated in the transit process. The chronic effects from these situations are cancer and respiratory effects e.g. asthma.

There has been a marked increase in use of pesticides by farmers in the north east of Scotland.   The bodies of dead animals (rabbits and a fox) have been found beside a stream which runs through land presently owned by the Forestry Commission, near Banchory, approximately 25 miles West of Aberdeen.   There have also been cases of human illness reported.   These cases are sporadic and geographically dispersed around the hinterland.

Two cases have broken out at one of the farms which is situated in close proximity to the Forestry Commission land.   The symptoms include, stomach pains, headache, sore throat, breathing difficulties, tightness in the chest and sore eyes. Other cases, approximately five in total, have differing symptoms and are less defined.   Two of these have taken place in Aberdeen, one in Ellon, one in Alford, and the last in Ballater.   The symptoms include stomach cramps, vomiting, headaches and some complain of muscle pain as well.

Doctors say that it appears to be a case of chemical poisoning but specific causes are unknown.   It is evident that the farm workers had been working with organic pesticides, spraying oil seed rape.

University of Aberdeen scientists are making tests on the stream water to try to identify the cause of the problem.   It is suspected that the chemical could be a herbicide like Benazalox which is commonly used in the production of oil seed rape, to eradicate broadleaved weeds like chickweed or mayweed.   They believe that a leaching action has taken place, precipitated by the recent rainfall and the water has been contaminated.

Scientists from Aberdeen University and The Robert Gordon University stress the need for extensive epidemiological tests to assess the correlations between the exposure and effects of the chemical.

Case 2: The Worsening of Respiratory Diseases Due to Atmospheric Pollution

Atmospheric pollution results from the mixture of a number of chemicals which are released into the air. These elements include sulphur, carbon, lead and nitrogen compounds. Toxic gases like nitrogen dioxide, sulphur dioxide and carbon monoxide have worried environmentalists and health scientists for some time due to their harmful properties.

During the combustion process in the engine, a reaction takes place between oxygen and nitrogen, where nitric oxide is produced. Nitric oxide is expelled through the exhaust and mixes with more atmospheric oxygen to produce nitrogen dioxide and the compound nitrogen tetraoxide (N_2O_4). The same occurs between sulphur and oxygen, producing compounds such as sulphur dioxide. Scientists believe that humans are affected by air pollution of this type, and more epidemiological studies are being carried out to prove this.

Nitric oxide is the main nitrogen component of car emission, which appears to be relatively harmless until it is oxidized and nitrogen dioxide is produced. Nitrogen dioxide is a toxic, brown gas, which has harmful effects on animals and vegetation, although when it is expelled from a vehicle's exhaust, it is colourless. Nitrogen dioxide has insiduous effects but can be measured easily. Nitrogen exists in the exhaust emitted from both diesel and non-diesel engines. The National Asthma Campaign state that NO_2 may irritate the airways and make them more sensitive to other triggers. It may also lower the body's defence mechanisms causing a reduced resistance to viral infections which can trigger asthma symptoms.

Tests have been carried out which indicate that sulphur dioxide is one factor which increases sensitisation to air particulates which act as irritants and cause asthma. Scientists are still trying to prove a direct cause and effect link between air pollution and respiratory diseases.

An eight year old girl from Dundee has died. The girl was an asthmatic, a bronchial condition which can be serious. Doctors who performed a post mortem believe that the cause of death could be anoxic asphyxiation from an asthma attack. However this report is not conclusive and they say that other factors probably contributed to the death.

The parents of the child strongly believe that one of the major elements which influenced the illness of their daughter was the substantial increase of traffic within the inner city of Dundee where they live. They intend to protest against the problem of increasing traffic by taking a petition to Downing Street, and have been rallying support amongst the other asthma sufferers in the area.

A study is being undertaken by the medical school of the University of Dundee, to ascertain whether people with chest and respiratory diseases who live beside or in close proximity to a major transport route or intensely built up area with increasing traffic problems, are deteriorating due to increased atmospheric pollution.

Health and medical scientists have stated that there is a slight correlation between air pollution and the worsening of respiratory diseases and that this has been defined by studies carried out into large conurbations where the volume of traffic is more intense.

Case 3: The Development of a Funicular Railway through the Cairngorm Mountain Range

During the 1960s a new road development and ski lifts were put into operation at Coire Cas on the Cairngorm. This progression brought jobs and therefore people into the area and the tourist industry benefitted from the increase in trade. This development was linked to the Aviemore village plans which was envisaged as a new all year tourist centre, and which was to include hotel complexes, retail outlets and leisure facilities.

Since its inception, ecologists and environmentalists have become concerned about the damage many of these developments are causing to the natural environment. Conservationists believe that the construction of the ski facilities, near Aviemore, resulted in more damage to the environment than was necessary. The heavy equipment used to prepare the ski runs has destroyed the thin alpine top soil which may take decades to recover. Such developments not only causes damage to vegetation and soils but can also affect a variety of habitats, for example, those of the birds and animals of the moor and mountain.

Approximately ten years ago, a proposal was put forward to extend the ski development into Lurchers' Gully. This was however unsuccessful because of the severe environmental damage which would occur as a result of this. At present no environmental groups want to see the existing skiing facilities reduced as this would result in loss of jobs for the community.   However, there is concern that the funicular proposal will cause greater conservation problems due to the increased numbers of visitors to one particular place and the implementation work itself which will cause more damage than installing ski tows.

The Cairngorm Chairlift Company have submitted a proposal outlining the development of a funicular railway through the Cairngorm ski area to replace the existing chairlift arrangement. It is estimated that the railway will run for approximately 1.9km, from the day lodge (which will be redesigned) to a new development (which will take the place of the Ptarmigan restaurant). The railway will climb to a height of 1,097 metres. It is estimated that the railway would have the capacity to carry 1,200 people per hour in the busy season and 500 who are seated at other times.

Members of the Scottish Wildlife and Countryside Link and the Save the Cairngorms Campaign have strong reservations about the impact of the development on the environment. Specifically, they have voiced concern about the substantial increases in numbers of people on the high plateau.

Steve Westbrook, an economist, commissioned by Scottish Wildlife and Countryside Link and The Save the Cairngorms Campaign to compile a financial analysis on the development, estimates that 175,000 people per year would use the railway outwith the skiing season, which is 125,000 more than use the chairlift at present. He states that an extra 50,000 people will be attracted to the area, which has implications for the tourism industry.

The funicular railway development is likely to provide the area with more jobs to cope with additional visitors. The area will also benefit from the increased amount of tourism which the venture is likely to attract. The converse side of the argument, highlights the fact that there will be a substantial increase in the amount of people on the hillside using the amenities. This will more than likely lead to conservation problems like soil erosion and habitat destruction.

The development is going to cause damage to the environment in its implementation stages and conservation groups are wondering whether it is a wise economic investment.

Case 4: Destruction of the Marine Environment by Overfishing

Resource Exploitation

In recent years, scientists have become concerned that the human exploitation of natural marine resources is damaging the environmental infrastructure of the sea. This applies not only to mineral resources like oil and gas, but to renewable resources e.g. fish and shell fish. These stocks are depleted where the rate of harvesting is greater than the rate at which the resource can reproduce or regenerate. Overfishing is, therefore, becoming one of today's most serious environmental problems. Overfishing can alter the environmental balance between species by interfering with the Eco-web structure.

Oceanic organisms provide 10-20% of world protein intake and sustain high levels of economic activity in Britain. In addition the fisheries industry can exist for an indeterminate period of time (if managed correctly) due to the fact that the resource is renewable.

> In 1988, global fishery harvests amounted to some 85 million tonnes (92 million tonnes if aquaculture), 15 million tonnes below the Food and Agriculture Organisation (FAO) estimated maximum global sustainable yield of 100 million tonnes. (The State of the Environment. OECD, 1991, p90)

The global concern at the moment is that resources are pitched below sustainable levels and consequently some of the more valuable fish stocks have been seriously depleted. Overfishing has occurred, historically, due to the increasing global need for protein and improvements in harvesting technology.

Overfishing is, therefore, linked inextricably to commercial activities. Consequently economic factors and environmental facts are often in conflict. Despite increasing restrictions on fishing, many species are becoming endangered by extinction, due to these measures.

Due to the increasing amount of fishing activity off the North East coast of Scotland, stocks of some species of fish have noticeably depleted. Marine scientists have reported that the North Sea is one of the most heavily used and exploited ocean environments. Ecologists are worried that certain species such as haddock and in particular cod, are in danger of being unable to reproduce sufficiently in order to survive. In the late seventies, supplies of herring were seriously depleted in the North Sea and the fish processing industries never fully recovered.

This will have serious consequences for the North East fishing industry and the economy of Aberdeen and its surrounding area. Unemployment in the area will increase dramatically. Fishing towns outside Aberdeen and Peterhead do not benefit from the oil industry nor from aquaculture so an alternative form of employment such as fish farming would not be appropriate.

Ecology and pollution experts are already concerned about the state of the North Sea. They have been monitoring it closely for industrial and municipal discharge, waste dumping and more specifically, petroleum hydrocarbons, trace metals and synthetic compounds. These factors combined have already contributed to the partial prohibition of species degeneration, overfishing will increase this to a higher level.

Case 5: Pollution in the North Sea

Marine pollution can have many different causes. Occurrences can take place from leakage of liquids eg fuel, lubricants or alcohol-based deicers. Often major oil pollution occurs as a result of a tanker disaster eg the Braer or Exxon Valdez. It is one of the most visible forms of pollution and also the most recognisable to the general public.

> Massive accidental spills can be lethal to many forms of marine life, including seabirds and marine mammals. More chronic forms of oil pollution in estuaries or near oil rigs can affect benthic populations, other resident biota, and critical habitats such as spawning grounds. (The State of the Environment. Paris: OCED, 1991, p73)

Oil used for fuel sometimes contains, PAH or polycyclic aromatic hydrocarbons (JetA1 fuel does not) which are poorly biodegradable and are classed as having toxic, mutagenic and carcinogenic effects. These hydrocarbons exist in crude oil and occur, therefore in fuel, petroleum and bitumen tar.

Aviation fuel is one of the lightest forms of the oil derivatives and it is highly flammable. The vapour from this product is heavier than air and oil producers suggest that a foam blanket be administered to the affected area to prevent ignition. Oil companies further suggest that in cases of spillages at sea or in any event whereby the product mixes with water, the spread of fuel should be prohibited by barriers and authorised dispersants used. A1 or Avtur, a type of jet fuel, will react strongly with oxidising agents, and thermal decomposition will cause smoke, and other hazardous gases. This product is inherently biodegradable, unlike some other oil based compounds. It is extremely toxic to aquatic life. when spilt on water a film of fuel is formed on the surface and this can physically damage marine organisms and can impair oxygen transfer. The fuel acts as a seal on the water and is preventing the oxygen exchange across water.

Scenario

A train travelling to Aberdeen to supply the airport with aviation fuel, is derailed crossing the Tay Rail Bridge. Three of the cars are carrying 31,000 tonnes of Avtur, a type of aviation turbine fuel, and two of which have become partially detached from the rest of the train. The fuel has begun leaking into the water - the Tay Firth.

The chemical breakdown of the fuel includes a number of different hydrocarbon compounds which is produced by the distillation of crude oil. The product releases fumes which should not be inhaled and on burning the fuel, the fumes become toxic.

Ecologists and zoologists are concerned over of the presence of a seal colony on the Firth and a large population of wintering ducks. The oil affects the insulation properties of mammals' skin and the creatures also ingest and inhale the fuel product. The oil is also accumulated by fish and consequently their flesh becomes tainted. The extent of the damage which the fuel may cause to marine and animal life is unknown at present. Scientists are monitoring levels of pollution as best they can by carrying out tests on water samples.

ScotRail have issued a statement saying that they are investigating the circumstances surrounding the incident.

Producers of the fuel warn personnel to avoid contact with the product. In the event of skin contamination the area should be washed with soap and water. Protective clothing should be worn at all times when handling the product.

Bibliography

Ainlay, S., "The Encounter with Phenomenology" in Hunter, J.D., (1986) *Making Sense of Modern Times: Peter L. Berger and the Vision of Interpretive Sociology.* London: Routledge and Kegan Paul., pp. 31-54.

Alston, P., (1991) Environment Online: The Greening Of Databases. *Database* (Oct), pp. 34-52.

Amor, A. J., (1991) Science Journalism Training in Asia. *Impact of Science on Society* 144, pp. 367-372.

Anthony, R., (1982) Polls, Pollution and Politics. *Environment* 24 (4), pp.14-20, 33-4.

Arundale, J., (1986) The Library Today. *Library Association Record* (Mar).

Arundale, J., (1989) Online and Newspapers. *ASLIB Information* 17 (11/12), pp 270-271.

Arundale, J., "The Importance of Information Management" in Eagle, S. (ed) (1991) *Information Sources for the Press and Broadcast Media.* London: Bowker Saur.

Arthur, C., (1991) Media Ecology as a Moral Priority. *The Month* 24 (Nov), pp.56-58.

Attwood, E.L., and Grotta, G.L., (1973) Socialization of News Values in Beginning Reporters. *Journalism Quarterly*, 50, pp. 759-761.

Bagdikian, B., (1984) How Technology Influences Journalism. *IEEE Spectrum*, pp 109-111.

Bagnall, N., (1991) *Newspaper Language.* London: Focal Press.

Bauer, R. "The Communicator and the Audience" in Dexter and White, (1964) *People, Society and Mass Communication.* New York: Macmillan.

Becker, L., (1987) *The Training and Hiring of Journalists in the United States.* Norwood: Ablex.

Bell, A., (1991) *The Language of News Media.* Oxford: Basil Blackwell.

Bell, A., (1994) Climate of Opinion: Public and Media Discourse on the Global Environment. *Discourse and Society* 5 (1), pp 33-64.

Berger, P., and Luckmann, T., (1991) *The Social Construction of Reality: A Treatise In the Sociology of Knowledge.* London: Penguin.

Bowers, D., (1967) A Report On Activity By Publishers In Directing Newsroom Decisions. *Journalism Quarterly* 44, Spring, pp. 43-52.

Boyd, A., (1992) *Broadcast Journalism: Techniques of Radio, and TV News.* Oxford: Focal Press.

Breed, W., (1955) Social Control in the Newsroom. *Social Forces* 33, May, pp. 326-335.

Breed, W., "Mass Communication and Sociocultural Integration" in Dexter and White, (1964) *People, Society and Mass Communication.* New York: Macmillan.

Briscoe, E., and Wall, C., (1992) Inexpensive News Sources. *Database*, February, pp. 28-35.

British Royal Commission on the Press in Dahlgren, P., and Sparks, C., (1991) *Communication and Citizenship: Journalism and the Public Sphere in the New Media Age.* London: Routledge.

Broder, D., (1987) *Behind the Front Page: A Candid Look at how the News is Made.* New York: Touchstone.

Brown, R., (1989) *Knowledge is Power: The Confusion of Information in Early America.* New York: Oxford University Press.

Bruck, P., (1982) The Social Production of Texts: On the Relation Production/Product in News Media. *Communication/Information* 4, pp. 92-124.

Burgess, J., (1990a) Making Sense of Environmental Issues and Landscape. Representations in the Media. *Landscape Research* 15 (3) pp. 7-11.

Burgess, J., (1990b) The Production and Consumption of Environmental Meanings in the Mass Media: A Research Agenda for the 1990s. *Transactions of the Institute of British Geographers*, New Series 15, pp. 139-161.

Burgess, J., [et al] (1991) Contested Meanings: The Consumption of News About Nature Conservation. *Media, Culture and Society* 13, pp. 499-519.

Burkhart, F.N., (1987) Experts and the Press Under Stress: Disaster Journalism Gets Mixed Reviews. International Journal of Mass Emergencies and Disasters 5, pp. 357-367.

Burkhart, F.N., (1991a) *Media, Emergency Warnings and Citizen Response.* Colorado: Westview Press.

Burkhart, F.N., (1991b) Journalists As Bureaucrats: Perceptions of "Social Responsibility". *International Journal of Mass Emergencies and Disasters 5*, pp. 357-367.

Burkhart, F.N., (1992) Media Functions and Environmental Management. *The Environmental Professional* 14 (1).

Campbell, F., (1995) The Analysis of Environmental Information: A Study of News. *New Library World*, 96 (1124), pp 32-33

Campbell, F., (1996) *The Analysis of Environmental Information: A study of the dissemination, mediation and interpretation of news.* Ph.D thesis, The Robert Gordon University, Aberdeen.

Campbell, F., (1997) The Journalistic Construction of News: Information Gathering. *New Library World* 98 (1133), pp 60-64.

Carey, J.W., (1989) *Communications As Culture: Essays on Media and Society.* London: Unwin and Hyman.

Carson, R., (1962) *Silent Spring.* London: Hamish Hamilton.

Cassidy, S., "The Environment and the Media: Two Strategies For Challenging Hegemony" in Hansen, A., (1993) *The Mass Media and Environmental Issues.* Leicester: Leicester University Press.

Christian, H., (1980) *The Sociology of Journalism and the Press.* Keele: University of Keele.

Clarke, A., (1991) *Making the News: A Focus For Change in the Role of Community Newspapers.* Glasgow: Community Service Groups in Scotland.

Clements, I., (1986) The Ravenous Half Shut Eye Manufacturing Bad News From Nowhere. *Media Information Australia* 39, pp. 5-8.

Clifford, J., (1986) *Writing Culture: The Poetics and Politics of Ethnography.* Berkley: University of California Press.

Cohen, E., (ed) (1992) *Philosophical Issues in Journalism.* New York; Oxford: Oxford University Press.

Cohen, S., and Young, J., (1973) *The Manufacture of News: A Reader.* Beverly Hills: Sage.

Collins, R., (1990) *Television: Policy and Culture.* London: Unwin and Hyman.

Coupland, N., [et al] (1991) *The Handbook of Miscommunication and Problematic Talk.* California: Sage.

Crowley, M., (1988) Optical Digital Disk Storage: An Application for News Libraries. *Special Libraries*, Winter, pp. 34-42.

Dahlgren, P., and Sparks, C., (1992) *Journalism and Popular Culture.* London: Sage.

Daley, P., and O'Neill, D., (1991) "Sad is too Mild a Word": Press Coverage of the Exxon Valdez Oil Spill. *Journal of Communication* 41 (4), pp. 43-57.

Davidson, A., (1990) *In the Wake of the Exxon Valdez: The Devastating Impact of the Alaska Oil Spill.* San Franicisco: Sierra Club Books.

DeFleur, M., and Dennis, E., (1988) Understanding Mass Communication. Boston: Houghton Mifflin.

DeMott, J., (1973) "Interpretive" News Stories Compared with "Spot" News. Journalism Quarterly 50, pp. 102-108.

DeSola Pool, I., and Shulman, I. "Newsmen's Fantasies, Audiences and Newswriting" in Dexter and White (1964) *People, Society and Mass Communication.* New York: Macmillan.

Douglas, J., (1971) *Understanding Everyday Life: Toward the Reconstruction of Sociological Knowledge.* London: Routledge and Kegan Paul.

Downs, A., (1972) Up and Down with Ecology - The "Issue Attention" Cycle. *Public Interest* 28, pp. 38-50.

Duffy, L.P., (1986) T.M.I. Accident and Recovery. *British Nuclear Energy Society Journal* 25 (4), pp. 199-215.

Duncan, M., (1993) Information Management In Newspapers. *ASLIB Information* 21 (5), May, pp. 208-209.

Dunwoody, S., (1978) From a Journalist's Perspective: Putting Content Into Mass Media Science Writing. *The English Journal* 67 (4), pp. 44-47.

180

Dunwoody, S., and Griffin, R., "Journalistic Strategies for Reporting Long-Term Environmental Issues: A Case Study of Three Superfund Sites" in Hansen, A., (ed) (1993) *The Mass Media and Environmental Issues.* Leicester: Leicester University Press.

Eagle, S., (ed) (1991) *Information Sources for Press and Broadcast Media.* London: Bowker-Saur.

Efron, E., (1971) *The News Twisters.* Los Angeles: Nash.

Einseidel, E.F., (1992) Framing Science and Technology in the Canadian Press. *Public Understanding of Science* 1 (1).

Einseidel, E. F., and Coughlan, E., "The Canadian Press and the Environment: Reconstructing a Social Reality" in Hansen, A., (1993) *The Mass Media and Environmental Issues.* Leicester: Leicester University Press.

Eldridge, J., (1993) *Getting the Message: News, Truth and Power.* London: Routledge.

Ericson, R., (1987) *Visualizing Deviance: A Study of News Organisation.* Milton Keynes: Open University Press.

Ericson, R., (1991) *Representing Order: Crime, Law and Justice in the News Media.* Milton Keynes: Open University Press.

Evans, H., (1979) *Newsman's English.* London: Heinemann.

Fanhnestock, J., (1986) Accommodating Science: The Rhetorical Life of Scientific Facts. *Written Communication* 3, pp. 275-296.

Fiske, J., (1987) *Television Culture.* London: Routledge.

Fost, D., (1990) Newspapers Enter the Age of Information. *American Demographics* 12, p. 14.

Fowler, R., (1991) *Language in the News: Discourse and Ideology in the Press.* London: Routledge.

Friedman, S., (ed) (1986) *Scientists and Journalists: Reporting Science As News.* New York: Macmillan.

Friedman, S., [et al] (1987) Reporting About Radiation: A Content Analysis of Chernobyl. *Journal of Communication*, pp. 58-79.

Funkhouser, G., (1973) Tailoring Science Writing to the General Audience. *Journalism Quarterly* 50, pp. 220-6.

Gamage, L., (1993) Meeting the Needs of Journalists. *Information World Review* June, pp. 8-9.

Gamson, W., and Modigliani, A., (1989) Media Discourse and Public Opinion on Nuclear Power: A Constructionist Approach. *American Journal of Sociology* 95 (1) July, pp. 1-37.

Gaunt, P., (1988) The Training Of Journalists In France, Britain and the United States. *Journalism Quarterly* 65, Fall, pp. 582-8.

Gaunt, P., (1990) *Choosing the News: The Profit Factor in News Selection.* New Jersey: Greenwood Press.

Geiber, W., "News Is What Newspapermen Make It" in Dexter, L., (1964) *People, Society and Mass Communication.* New York: Free Press.

181

Glynn, C.J., (1988) Perceptions of Communication Use in Science Policy Decision Making. *Journalism Quarterly* 65, spring, pp. 54-61.

Goldsmith, F. B., and Warren, A., (eds) (1992) *Conservation in Progress.* John Wiley.

Grampian Television (1991) *An Application for the Seven Day Regional Licence to Provide a Television Broadcasting Service on Channel 3 in the North of Scotland.* Sections A and B. (May).

Greenaway, J., (1992) *Deciding Factors in British Politics.* London: Routledge.

Greenberg, D.W., (1985) Staging Media Events to Achieve Legitimacy: A Case Study of Britain's Friends of the Earth. *Political Communication and Persuasion* 2 (4), pp. 347-62.

Greenberg, M., [et al] (1989) Risk, Drama and Geography in Coverage of Environmental Risk by Network TV. *Journalism Quarterly* 66 (2), pp. 267-276.

Grunig, L.A., (ed) (1989) *Environmental Activism Revisited: The Changing Nature of Communication Through Organisational Public Relations, Special Interest Groups and the Mass Media.* Ohio: North American Association for Environmental Education.

Gundlach, E., (1977) Oil Tanker Disasters. *Environment* 19 (9), pp. 16-20, 25-27.

Hackett, R., (1984) Decline of a Paradigm? Bias and Objectivity in News Media Studies. *Critical Studies in Mass Communication* 1 (3), pp. 229-59.

Hage, J., and Aiken, M., (1969) Routine Technology, Social Structure and Organisational Goals. *Administrative Science Quarterly* 14 (3), pp. 366-78.

Halberstam, J., "A Prolegomenon for a Theory of News" in Cohen, E., (ed) (1992) *Philosophical Issues in Journalism.* New York; Oxford: Oxford University Press.

Hall, S., (1970) A World At One With Itself. *New Society* 18 June.

Hall, S., (1978) *Policing the Crisis: Mugging, the State and Law and Order.* London: Routledge.

Hancock-Beaulieu, M., (ed) (1992) *Information Systems for End-Users: Research and Development Issues.* Taylor Graham.

Hansen, A. (1990a) "The News Construction of the Environment" in Linne, O., and Hansen, A., *News Coverage of the Environnment: A Comparative Study of Journalistic Practices and Television Presentation in Danmarks Radio and the BBC.* Danmarks Radio: Research Report No 1B/90, pp. 4-63.

Hansen, A., (1990b) Socio-political Values Underlying Media Coverage of the Environment. *Media Development* 37 (2), pp. 3-6.

Hansen, A., (1990c) *The News Construction of the Environment.* Centre for Mass Communication Research.

Hansen, A., (1991) The Media and the Social Construction of the Environment. *Media, Culture and Society* 13, pp. 443-458.

Hansen, A., (1993) *The Mass Media and Environmental Issues.* Leicester: Leicester University Press.

Harris, G., and Spark, D., (1993) *Practical Newspaper Reporting.* London: Focal Press

Hartley, J., (1982) *Understanding News.* London: Methuen.

Hart, J., (1990) The Classroom and the Newsroom: Missed Opportunities For Journalism Education. *Newspaper Research Journal* 11.4, Fall, pp. 38-50.

Hartley, J., (1992) *The Politics of Pictures.* London: Routledge.

Heaney, M., (1986) BBC Scotland Library Services. *Scottish Library Association News* 194, July/Aug, pp. 16-17, 19.

Heeter, C., [et al] (1989) Agenda Setting By Electronic Text News. *Journalism Research,* pp. 714-18.

Hesketh, B., (1993) *An Introduction to ENG.* London: Focal Press.

Hetherington, A., (1985) *News, Newspapers and Television.* London: Macmillan.

Hightower, P., (1984) The Influence of Training on Taking and Judging Photographs. *Journalism Quarterly* 61, Autumn, pp. 682-6.

Hogwood, B. W., (1992) *Ups and Downs: Is There an Issue-Attention Cycle in Britain?* Glasgow: Department of Government, University of Strathclyde.

Hogwood, B., and Gunn, L., (1984) *Policy Analysis For the Real World.* New York: Oxford University Press.

Howenstine, E., (1987) Environmental Reporting: A Shift from 1970-1982. *Journalism Quarterly* 64 (4), pp. 842-6.

Hodgson, F.W., (1993) *Modern Newspaper Practice.* London: Focal Press.

Hodgson, F.W., (1987) *Subediting: A Handbook of Modern Newspaper Editing and Production.* London: Focal Press.

Hughes, H., (1980) News And The Human Interest Story. University of Chicago Press.

Hunter, J.D., (1986) *Making Sense of Modern Times: Peter L. Berger and the Vision of Interpretive Sociology.* London: Routledge and Kegan Paul.

Ishikawa, S., (1990) Media Generated Minorities: The Role of Japan's Mass Media In Pollution Disasters. Studies of Broadcasting, March, pp. 105-20.

Jacobson, T., (1989) Commercial Databases and Reporting. Newspaper Research Journal 10 (2), pp. 16-25.

Jansma, P.E., (1993) Reading About the Environment. Englewood, Co.: Libraries Unlimited, Inc.

Jensen, K.B., (1981) *Making Sense of the News: Towards a Theory and an Empirical Model of Reception for the Study of Mass Communication.* Aarhus University Press.

Jones, B., (1987) Expanding News Coverage. *Journal of Information Science* (13), pp. 313-316.

Jones, G., (1978) Sources and Selection of Scientific Material for Newspapers and Radio Programmes. *Journal of Research Communication Studies* III, pp. 69-82.

Joseph, R., (1993) How Indian Journalists Use Libraries. *Information Development* 9 (1/2), pp. 70-75.

Keeter, S., (1984) Problematic Pollution Polls: Validity in the Measurement of Public Opinion on Environmental Issues. *Political Methodology,* 10, pp. 267-292.

183

Kessel, H., (1985) Changes in Environmental Awareness: A Comparative Study of the FRG, England and the USA. *Land Use Policy* 2 (April), pp. 103-113.

Kerr, R., (1988) Is the Greenhouse Here? *Science* 239, pp. 559-561

Khoo, T., (1986) Technology and its Impact on Journalism. *The New Information Professionals*, September, pp. 106-115.

Koch, N., (1990) New Beat in the News Room. *Channels* (May), p. 22.

Koch, T., (1990) *The News as Myth: Fact and Context in Journalism.* New Jersey: Greenwood Press.

Koch, T., (1991) *Journalism in the 21st Century: Online Information, Electronic Databases and the News.* Twickenham: Adamantine Press.

Lacey, C., (1993) The Press and Public Access To The Environment and Development Debate. *The Sociological Review* 41 (2), pp, 207-243.

Lane, J., (1993) *Public Sector: Concepts, Models and Approaches.* London: Sage.

Learning for Life: A National Strategy for Environmental Education in Scotland. (1993) Edinburgh: Scottish Office

Lee, J.A., (1989) Waging the Seal War in the Media: Towards a Content Analysis of Moral Communication. *Canadian Journal of Communication* 14 (1), pp. 37-55.

Leonard, T., (1992) Databases in the Newsroom. *Online,* May, pp. 62-65.

Levinton, J., (1990) Electronic News Delivery. *Special Libraries*, pp. 180-182.

Lewenstein, B.V., (1992) *When Science Meets The Public.* Washington: American Association For The Advancement of Science.

Lindell, M., (1990) Effects of Chernobyl Accident on Public Perceptions of Nuclear Power Plant Accidents Risks. *Risk Analysis* 9, pp. 211-219.

Lodziak, C., (1987) *The Power of Television: A Critical Appraisal.* London: Pinter.

Love, A., (1990) The Production of Environmental Meanings in the Media: A New Era. *Media Education Journal,* pp. 18-20.

Lowe, P., and Morrison, D., (1984) Bad News or Good News: Environmental Politics and the Mass Media. *Sociological Review*, 32 (1), pp. 75-90.

Lowe, P., and Goyder, J., (1983) *Environmental Groups in Politics.* London; Boston: Allen and Unwin.

Luckmann, T., (1972) Review of Understanding Everyday Life. *Contemporary Society* 1 (1), pp. 30-32.

Luke, T.W., (1987) Chernobyl: The Packaging of a Transnational Ecological Disaster. *Critical Studies in Mass Communication* 4, pp. 351-75.

Luter, J., (1983) Training Chinese Journalists At The University of Hawaii. *Language Learning and Communication* 2 (1), pp. 93-95.

MacGill, S., (1987) *The Politics of Anxiety: Sellafield's Cancer-Link Controversy.* London: Pion.

MacGuen, M., and Coombs, S., (1981) *More Than News: Media Power in Public Affairs.* Beverly Hills: Sage.

184

McCormick, J., (1992) *The Global Environmental Movement: Reclaiming Paradise.*

McDowell, E. (1993) *The Scottish Environmental Movement: The Impact of Values and Trends Which Shaped the Movement's Historical Development.* Unpublished paper, School of Public Administration and Law, The Robert Gordon University, Aberdeen.

McGehan, F.B., (1979) *Interpreting the Scientific Paper For the Trade Press.* Washington, DC: National Bureau of Standards.

McNair, B., (1994) News and Journalism in the UK: A Textbook. London: Routledge.

McQuail, D., (1993) *Media Performance: Mass Communication and the Public Interest.* California, Newbury Park: Sage.

McQuail, D., and Windahl, S., (1993) *Communication Models: For the Study of Mass Communication.* New York: Longman.

Manoff, R., and Schudson, M., (1987) *Reading the News.* New York: Panethon.

Mansfield, J., (1991) *News! News! News Gathering For Television.* Borehamwood: BBC TV Training.

Marsh, H., (1973) How Journalism Teachers View Media News Performance. *Journalism Quarterly* 50, pp. 137-139.

Mayer, M., (1993) *Making News.* Doubleday and Company.

Media and the Environment: A Workshop Report. Paisley: SEEC Occasional Paper No 1.

Meltzner, A.J., (1981) The Communication of Scientific Information To the Wider public. *Minerva* 17 (3), pp. 27-41.

Milton, K., (1991) Interpreting Environmental Policy: A Social Scientific Approach. *Environment* 18 (Spring), pp. 4-17.

Molotch, H., and Lester, M., (1975) Accidental News: The Great Oil Spill as Local Occurrence and National Event. *American Journal of Sociology* 81 (2), pp. 235-360.

Moore, M., (ed) (1989) *Health Risks and the Press: Perspectives on Media Coverage of Risk Assessment and Health.* Washington: The Media Institute.

Morgan, R., (1988) *The Media and the Environment: A Study of the Treatment of Environmental News Issues With Specific Reference to British Daily Newspapers.* Unpublished PhD Thesis.

Morris, B., (1986) *Images: Illusion and Reality.* Canberra: Australian Academy of Science.

Morris, J., (1973) Newsmen's Interviewing Techniques and Attitudes toward Interviewing. *Journalism Quarterly* 50, pp. 539-542, 548.

Musburger, R., (1991) *Electronic News Gathering: A Guide to E.N.G.* Boston, Mass.; London: Focal Press.

Negrine, R., and Papathanassopoulos, S., (1990) *The Internationalization of Television.* New York: Pinter.

Negrine, R., (1994) *Politics and the Mass Media in Britain.* London: Routledge.

Nelkin, D., (1987) *Selling Science: How the Press Covers Science and Technology.* New York: Freeman.

Neuwirth, K., (1988) The Effect of Electronic News Sources on Selection and Editing of News. *Journalism Quarterly* 65 (1), pp. 85-94.

Nev, M., (1988) Resources of Newspaper Libraries. *Texas Library Journal* 64, pp. 58-60.

Nicholas, D., [et al] (1987a) Information storage and Retrieval in UK National Newspapers: Some Effects of Change. *Journal of Librarianship* 19 (2), April, pp. 71-88.

Nicholas, D., [et al] (1987b) Information Storage and Retrieval in UK National Newspapers. *Online Review* 11 (4), pp. 219-238.

Nimmo, D., and Combs, J.E., (1985) *Nightly Horrors: Crisis Coverage in Television Network News.* Knoxville: University of Tennessee Press.

The Oil Spill Problem. (1971) Washington DC: Office of Science and Technology.

Ojala, M., (1991) Online Broadcast News: From Television Screen to Computer Screen. *Database*, April, pp. 33-40.

Orna, E., (1990) *Practical Information Policies: How to Manage Information Flow in Organisations.* London: Gower.

Ostman, R., and Parker, J., (1987) Impact of Education, Age, Newspapers and Television on Environmental Knowledge, Concerns and Behaviors. *Journal of Environmental Education* 19 (1), pp. 3-9.

Parsigian, E. K., (1987) News Reporting: Method in the Midst of Chaos. *Journalism Quarterly* 64 (4), pp. 721-730.

Patrick, A., (1990) *Notes on Newswriting.* Unpublished paper, City University, London.

Patterson, P., "Reporting Chernobyl: Cutting the Government Fog to Cover the Nuclear Cloud" in Waters, L., (ed) (1989) *Bad Tidings: Communication and Catastrophe.* Hillsdale, NJ: Lawrence Erlbaum Associates.

Philo, G., (1990) *Seeing and Believing: The Influence of Television.* London: Routledge.

Pierce, J., (1990) Media Reliance and Public Images of Environmental Politics in Ontario and Michigan. *Journalism Quarterly* 67, Winter, pp. 838-42.

Protess, D.L., (1987) The Impact of Investigative Reporting on Public Opinion and Policy Making Targeting Toxic Waste. *Public Opinion Quarterly* 51, pp. 166-185.

Rachline, A., (1988) *News as Hegemonic Reality.* NY: Praeger.

Robinson, J., and Levy, M., (1986) *The Main Source: Learning from Television News.* Beverly Hills: Sage.

Rogers, E.M., (1987) *Diffusion of Innovations.* New York: Free Press.

Rubin, D., (1987) How the News Media Reported on T.M.I. and Chernobyl. *Journal of Communication* 37 (3), pp. 42-57.

Ryan, M., (1991) Risk Information for Public Consumption: Print Media Coverage of Two Risky Situations. *Health Education Quarterly* 18 (3), pp. 375-390.

Salmon, P., (1988) Flickering Images of Green. *Environment Now* 1 (Feb), pp. 24-25.

Salwen, M., (1988) Effect of Accumulation of Coverage on Issue Salience in Agenda Setting. *Journalism Quarterly* 65, spring, pp. 100-6

Sandman, P., (1987) Risk Communication: Facing Public Outrage. *EPA Journal*, pp. 21-22.

Sandman, P., [et al] (1988) *Environmental Risk and the Press.* New York: Freeman.

Scottish Office (1993) *Learning For Life.* Edinburgh: Scottish Office.

Sellers, L., (1973) Environment and the Mass Media. *The Journal of Environmental Education* 5 (1), pp. 51-57.

Semonche, B., (1993) *News Media Libraries: A Management Handbook.* Westport, Connecticut: Greenwood Press.

Shawcross, W., (1984) *The Quality of Mercy.* Touchstone.

Shoemaker, P.J., (1991) *Mediating the Message: Theories of Influence on Mass Media Content.* New York: Longman.

Sibbison, J., (1988) Dead Fish and Red Herrings: How the EPA Pollutes the News. *Columbia Journalism Review* 27, Nov/Dec, pp. 25-8.

Sigelman, L., (1973) An Organisational analysis of News Reporting. *American Journal of Sociology* 79 (1).

Singer, E., (1990) A Question of Accuracy: How Do Journalists and Scientists Report Research on Hazards. *Journal of Communication* 40 (4), pp. 102-116.

Sito, C.L., (1990) *Deciding Who's News: A Content Analysis of Disaster, National and International News in Two Elite Newspapers from 1985-1989.* Unpublished Masters Thesis.

Sood, R., [et al] (1987) How the News Media Operate in Natural Disasters. *Journal of Communication* 37 (3), pp. 27-41.

Spencer, P., (1990) *White Silk and Black Tar: A Journal of the Alaskan Oil Spill.*

Stanbridge, R., (1992) Journalists Begin to Embrace Online Databases. *Information World Review*, December, pp. 46-48.

Stare, J., (1987) Some Press Coverage Does Not Meet Scientific Standards. *Nutrition Today* (May/June), p. 44.

Steinhart, C., and Steinhart, J., (1972) *Blowout: A Case Study of the Santa Barbara Oil Spill.* California: Duxbury Press.

Stephens, M., and Edison, N., (1982) News Media Coverage of Issues During the Accident at Three-Mile Island. *Journalism Quarterly* (Summer), pp. 199-204, 259.

Stocking, S. H., (1989) *How Do Journalists Think?: A Proposal For The Study of Cognitive Bias in Newsmaking.* Indiana: Bloomington.

Stocking, H., (1990) The Greening of the Press. *Columbia Journalism Review* Nov/Dec, pp. 37-44.

Stoss, F., (1991) Environment Online: The Greening of Databases. *Database* (Aug), pp. 13-27.

Stover, M., (1991) Newspapers on CD-ROM. *CD-ROM Professional*, November, pp. 100-104.

Strothoff, G. C., [et al] (1985) Media Roles in a Social Movement: A Model of Ideology Diffusion. *Journal of Communication* 35 (2), pp. 134-53.

Tiffen, R., (1989) *News and Power.* Sydney: Allen and Unwin.

Timberlake, L., (1989) Freedom of Information on the Environment. *Index on Censorship* (Jul/Aug), pp. 6-7.

Tuchman, G., (1969) *News, The Newsman's Reality.* Unpublished PhD Thesis, Brandeis University.

Tuchman, G., (1972) Objectivity as Strategic Ritual: An Examination of Newsmen's Notions of Objectivity. *American Journal of Sociology* 77 (4), pp. 660-79.

Tuchman, G., (1973) The Technology of Objectivity. *Urban Life and Culture* 2, (April).

Tuchman, G., (1978) *Making News: A Study in the Construction of Reality.* New York: Free Press.

Tuchman, G., (1982) Making News By Doing Work. *American Journal of Sociology* 79 (1), pp. 130-1.

Van Dijk, T. A., (1988) *News Analysis: Case Studies of International and National News in the Press.* Hillsdale, NJ: Erlbaum.

Venables, J., (1993) *What Is News?* London: Elm Publications.

Vergusson, C., (1985) A Library in the Media. *Audio Visual Librarian*, pp. 71-75.

Walters, L. M., [et al] (1988) *Bad Tidings: Communication and Catastrophe.* Hillsdale: L. Erlbaum.

Wasco, J., and Mosco, V., (1992) *Democratic Communications in the Information Age.* Toronto: Garamond Press.

Watson, J., and Hill, A., (1990) *A Dictionary of Communication and Media Studies.* New York: Routledge. 3rd Ed.

Weaver, D., (1991) *The American Journalist: A Portrait of US News People and their Work.* Indiana: Indiana University Press.

Westin, A.V., (1982) *Newswatch: How TV decides the News.* New York: Simon and Schuster.

White, D.M., "The 'Gatekeeper': A Case Study in the Selection of News" in Dexter and White (1964) *People, Society and Mass Communication.* New York: Macmillan.

Wilkes, J., (1978) Science Writing: Who? What? How? *The English Journal* 67 (4), pp. 56-60.

Wilkins, L., (1987) Risk Analysis and the Construction of News. *Journal of Communication* 37, pp. 80-92.

Wilkins, L. and Patterson, P., (1991) *Risky Business: Communicating Issues of Science, Risk and Public Policy.* New York: Greenwood Press.

Wilkinson, D., and Waterton, J., (1991) *Public Attitudes to the Environment In Scotland.* Edinburgh: Scottish Office.

188

Williams, P., (1990) *The Computerised Newspaper: A Practical Guide For System Users.* London: Heinemann.

Willis, J., (1991) *The Shadow World: Life Between the News Media and Reality.* New York: Praeger.

Wills, J., and Warner, K., (1993) *Innocent Passage: The Wreck of the Tanker Braer.* Edinburgh: Mainstream Publishing.

Winsten, J.A., (1985) Science and the Media: The Boundaries of Truth. *Health Affairs* 6, pp. 5-23.

Wright, S., and Wright, L., (1993) *Scientific and Technical Translation.* Amsterdam: John Benjamins.

Young, J., (1990) *Post Environmentalism.* London: Belhaven.

Index

scientific variables in, 143,
147-148
source variables in, 142, 146
crime, 22

deadlines (for journalists), 70,
130-132, 151, 156-157,
167
disaster
see Braer disaster
see eco-incident
see environmental disaster
discourse analysis, iv
see content analysis
distortion
see bias
see objectivity
see subjectivity
Dundee, 113

eco-incident, 41-42, 73-75, 84,
110, 114, 117, 172
see also environmental
disaster
editors
control and influence over
environmental news, 14, 32,
50, 57-60, 67, 70, 76, 97-
98, 100-101, 117, 131,
136, 138, 150, 159, 164,
167, 173
editorial rules 66-72
education of journalists
51-54
see also training
electronic news sources, 10,
31, 35, 37, 118-119, 174
see also media library
emergency services (as sources
of news), 35
environmental correspondent,
74-79, 85, 90-91, 127,
147-149, 152, 163, 174
environmental disaster, 13-15,
22-23, 35-38, 42, 64, 73,
75, 80-84, 87, 93, 100-
101, 110-115, 125, 130,
161-163
see also Braer disaster

see also Exxon Valdez
see also eco-incident
see also environmental
disaster
see also negativity
see also news stories,
dramatic emphasis
environmental groups, 1,4,6,
35, 56. 92-93, 99, 111,
114, 127-129
see also environmentalism
environmental impact, 75, 110
environmental information, I-
iii, 2-6, 108, 131-132,
160-161, 170-172
and news construction
model, 28-38
pluralistic and complex, 2,
21, 124, 132, 175
environmental issues, 23, 33,
37, 73, 76
environmental news, 11-13
'hard' news 76, 81-84, 89,
93-94, 99, 102-104, 154
see also news stories
news construction model,
28-38
see also news process
see also news stories
'soft' news, 78-79, 82-85,
94, 154
see also news stories
environmental politics, 3, 12
see also political agenda
environmentalism, 2, 92, 114
Ericson, R, 8-9, 28, 36
ethics, 123
ethnocentrism, 87, 105
ethnographic research, iv, 176
evaluation of news, 73-207
see also rules, evaluative
experts, 3, 11, 21, 31, 35, 44-
47, 66, 113-115, 121-
130, 163
see also environmental
correspondents
scientists
subject specialists